A noren curtain traditionally placed in front of shop doors. The characters on the noren, Dōzo [Dohh-zoh], mean Please [Come In]!

AMAZING JAPAN – 2

Other Books by the Author
[a partial listing]

[Books on Japan]
Japanese Etiquette & Ethics in Business
Japan's Business Code Words
The Japanese Have a Word for It!
Mistress-Keeping in Japan
Exotic Japan—The Sensual & Visual Pleasures
Discovering Cultural Japan
Business Guide to Japan
Japanese in Plain English
Survival Japanese
Instant Japanese
Japan Made Easy—All You Need to Know to Enjoy Japan
Dining Guide to Japan
Shopping Guide to Japan
Etiquette Guide to Japan—Know the Rules that Make the Difference
Japan's Cultural Code Words
Japan Unzipped—The Japan behind the Cherry Blossom Façade, (e-book)
KATA—The Key to Understanding & Dealing with the Japanese
Speak Japanese Today—A Little Language Goes a Long Way!
The Japanese Samurai Code—Classic Strategies for Success
Japan Unmasked—The Character & Culture of the Japanese
Elements of Japanese Design—Understanding & Using Japan's Classic *Wabi-Sabi-Shibui* Concepts
Sex and the Japanese—The Sensual Side of Japan
Samurai Strategies—42 Secret Martial Arts from Musashi's "Book of Five Rings"

AMAZING JAPAN – 3

Why the Japanese are a Superior People—The Advantages of Using Both Sides of Your Brain!

[Books on China]
The Chinese Mind—Understanding Traditional Chinese Beliefs and Their Influence on Contemporary Culture
Chinese Etiquette & Ethics in Business
China's Cultural Code Words [Key Chinese Terms that Reveal the Culture and Mindset of the Chinese]
Chinese in Plain English
Survival Chinese
Instant Chinese
Etiquette Guide to China—Know the Rules that Make the Difference

[Books on Korea]
Korean Business Etiquette
Korean in Plain English
Korea's Business & Cultural Code Words
Etiquette Guide to Korea— Know the Rules that Make the Difference
Instant Korean
Survival Korean

[Books on Mexico]
Why Mexicans Think & Behave the Way They Do—The Cultural Factors that Created the Character & Personality of the Mexican People
Mexican Cultural Code Words [hard-cover]
There's a Word for It in Mexico [paperback]

[Other Titles]
Which Side of Your Brain Am I Talking To? – The Advantages of Using Both Sides of Your Brain!
How to Measure the Sexuality of Men & Women by Their Facial Features

<u>AMAZING JAPAN – 4</u>

Samurai Principles & Practices that will Help Preteens &
Teens in School, Sports, Social Activities
& Choosing Careers
Romantic Hawaii—Sun, Sand, Surf & Sex
Romantic Mexico—The Image & the Realities
The Sensual Side of the Orient—A Traveler's
Arm-Chair Guide, (e-book)
Asian Face Reading—Unlock the Secrets Hidden
in the Human Face
Once a Fool—From Japan to Alaska by
Amphibious Jeep

*Various titles published in Chinese, Czech, French,
German, Hebrew, Italian, Indonesian, Japanese, Polish,
Portuguese, Russian & Spanish.*

AMAZING JAPAN – 5

Amazing Japan!

[Miwaku no Nihon!]
[Me-wah-kuu no Nee-hoan!]

Why Japan is one of the World's Most Intriguing Countries!

Boyé Lafayette De Mente

PHOENIX BOOKS / PUBLISHERS
ISBN: 0-914778-29-3
Copyright © 2009 by Boyé Lafayette De Mente.
All rights reserved worldwide.

AMAZING JAPAN – 6

CONTENTS

[1]
Japan is
World-Class Travel Mecca

[2]
Japan's Appeal to Foreigners
Exotic and Sensual

[3]
More Secrets of Japan's Appeal
to Westerners

[4]
Aesthetic Side of Japanese Culture
Has Powerful Influence

[5]
Japan's Amazing Traditions
Of Recreational Travel

[6]
Japan's Shoguns Created
The World's First Travel Industry

[7]
The Amazing Traditions
Of Goodwill & Service

[8]
Honored Guest Syndrome
Makes Japanese Great Hosts

[9]
Special Amenities Come with
Life in Japan

[10]
Getting the Feel of the Real Japan

AMAZING JAPAN – 8

[11]
In Japan it's Not All
Raw Fish, Rice & Noodles!

[12]
Restaurants in Japan the Epitome
of Good Taste

[13
Fast Foods Invented in Japan Ages Ago

[14]
Japan's Izakaya Outdo
Ireland's Pubs

[15]
Beverage of the Gods
Has Long History

[16]
ENKAI !
How to Party Japanese Style!

[17]
Visitors Can Enjoy
Japan's Most Popular Pastime

[18]
"Vistas Fit for The Eyes of Kings"

[19]
Japan's Hot Spring Spas
Add Erotic Spice to Life

[20]
Vacationers, Honeymooners,
Lovers, Fugitives Flock to Hot Springs

[21]
The Story Behind
Japan's Famous "Bullet Trains"

[22]
Japan's Amazing Abundance
of Annual Festivals

AMAZING JAPAN – 9

[23]
Celebrating New Year's
the Japanese Way
[24]
The Wonder that Was
(and is) Tokyo!
[25]
View from the Top of Tokyo
[26]
The Wonder that Was
(and is) Kyoto!
[27]
Playing the Geisha Game
in Present-Day Japan
[28]
The Influence of "Characters"
On Japan's Culture
[29]
Visitors Can Watch
Svelte Female "Samurai"
[30]
Travelers Can Max Out
On Japanese Manga
[31]
Japan's Amazing
Earthquake Technology
[32]
"Just in Time"
System Only Half of Story
[33]
Secrets of Japan's
Award-Winning Designs
[34]
In Japan Good Design is Everywhere!

[35]
Look Out Bill and Steve!
Here Comes Kohei and Genri!
[36]
Live Long and Prosper
In Japan's "Shangri La"
[37]
Japan's Martial Arts
Build Self-Confidence, Courage
[38]
The Story behind Japan's
Notorious Ninja
[39]
A Japanese Custom worth Emulating
[40]
Amazing Ainu –
The "Indians" of Japan
[41]
KARAOKE:
[kah-rah-oh-kay]
Somebody Really Invented It!
[42]
Japan's Guest House is A Sight to See!
[43]
Japan is Number One in Street Strolling
[44]
Japan Remains Safe Haven
For Foreign Travelers
[45]
Lowdown on the Cost of Doing Japan!

Preface

The Unknown Country!

JAPAN WAS totally unknown to Europeans until 1543. That fateful year a Chinese junk with a number of Portuguese traders aboard was driven by a typhoon onto the shores of the tiny island of *Tanega* (Tah-nay-gah) 25 miles (40 km) south of Kyushu, one of the four main islands of the Japanese archipelago. [The island of Tanega is now the launch center for Japan's space activities.]

These traders—who quickly introduced the Japanese to guns, tobacco and venereal disease—returned some months later to the Portuguese settlement of Macao on the southeast coast of China, where they spread the news of their accidental discovery.

Within a short time, other European traders and the inevitable missionaries soon began flocking to Japan—the traders seeking more business opportunities and the missionaries seeking religious converts.

The Europeans found Japan and its unique culture both fascinating and revolting. This fascination and revulsion was to grow over the coming decades and centuries, but for most Westerners throughout this long period the fascinating elements of Japan's culture were far stronger than its repulsive side.

Despite the fact that some of the early foreigners who took up residence in Japan grew to hate the Japanese, many of them remained there for long periods of time—sometimes for life—because there was something about the culture that kept them there despite their feelings.

The negative reaction of these Westerners no doubt began as emotional responses to some of the attitudes and behavior of the Japanese that they regarded as irrational and sometimes inhumane.

However, as time went by, aspects of the *Japanese Way* that these people found pleasing and satisfying began to overshadow the negative factors. Their various dislikes did not disappear but were generally expressed only in a constantly critical attitude.

Following the end of World War II in 1945 many Westerners who became involved with Japan predicted that the country would never amount to anything—that the people were simply not capable of creating a modern society.

The more successful the Japanese were over the next several decades, the more lame the criticisms of this group, until finally their animosity began to dissipate and be replaced by grudging respect.

On the other and much larger side of this encounter with Japan were those people who found living there an extraordinarily satisfying experience—not only in their personal one-on-one interaction with individual Japanese, but also in the pleasure and satisfaction they got from the traditional arts, crafts, food, efficiency and order that were an integral part of the culture.

Not surprisingly to those who are familiar with Asia cultures, much of the attraction that Japan held—and still holds—for Westerners was both overtly and covertly sensual in nature.

In this collection of essays I have attempted to identify and comment on some of the elements in Japanese culture that I believe make Japan one of the most fascinating countries in the world, and provide some incentive for those who have not yet experienced Japan to put it high on their list of places to visit.

Boyé Lafayette De Mente

[1]
Japan is World-Class Travel Mecca

SHORTYLY AFTER the turn of the 20th century a movement began to redefine Japan's image as a travel destination -- to take it well beyond the traditional symbols of Mt. Fuji, geisha and the country's famous "Bullet Trains." These images were not being discarded or down-played. They remained powerful attractions. But there is much more to Japan than these famous symbols.

Leaders in this movement pointed to the world image of France as the Mecca of food lovers and high fashions; to the image of Spain for its traditions of music, romance, bullfights and sunny beaches; and to the United States for its image of wide open spaces, Western cowboys, Hollywood films, titans of finance and industry, and such attractions as the Grand Canyon, gambling casinos, theme parks, and the freewheeling social behavior of Americans- all of which have made these countries favored travel destinations.

Other popular destinations such as China, England, Greece, Italy and Mexico have their own unique, deeply embedded, positive images that derive from their culture and history. But the image of Japan is not as clear, not as familiar, and not as appealing...for both historical and cultural reasons.

One obvious reason for the vague and highly selective image of Japan is because the country was virtually isolated from the most of the rest of the world until the last decades of the 19th century, and until the mid-20th century it was seen as a country ruled by militarists who were determined to dominate East and Southeast Asia.

Another equally obvious reason why the rest of the world has generally not been interested in Japan as a travel destination is the fact that—with the exception of Korea and China—there were few if any historical, racial and cultural ties…and in the case of these two neighboring countries, the depredations against them by the Japanese military in earlier years created a reservoir of distrust and enmity that people who lived through those times cannot forget.

But times have changed dramatically. The warrior code and feudalistic form of government that controlled the lives of the Japanese for centuries ended in 1945. With personal freedom for the first time in their history, the long oppressed character and qualities of ordinary Japanese—distinguished by an extraordinary degree of honesty, diligence, order, efficiency, hospitality, friendliness, and work ethic—came to the fore.

These characteristics played a vital role in the astounding emergence of Japan as the second largest economy in the world, surpassed only by the behemoth of the United States-and they are now among the elements that make Japan—unbeknown to many—one of the most attractive travel destinations in the world.

Over and above the stunning scenic beauty of the Japanese islands, the historical artifacts derived from Shinto and Buddhist influences, and the exotic Oriental elements in the traditional arts, crafts and customs of the Japanese, there is another factor that sets the Japanese apart and gives life in the country—for residents and visitors alike—a special ambiance.

This special factor is the character and behavior of the people themselves, especially their attitude and behavior toward clients and customers in business, and toward guests in the hospitality and travel industries.

In no country is the solicitous caring for guests and travelers more highly developed than in Japan. It is, in fact, an art that has been an integral part of the culture for generations, refined and practiced until it became a part of the national character.

When this element is added to the sense of security and the unsurpassed physical convenience and comfort of traveling in Japan—the hotels, the inns, the trains and subways—and to the availability of gourmet quality food from the around the world, an entertainment industry that is second to none, and endless shopping opportunities, you have a travel destination that is second to none.

All levels of the Japanese government from the Prime Minister on down, along with the public at large and businesses in general, have become acutely aware of the importance of tourism—economically, politically and culturally—and have joined in efforts to showcase the real Japan—the unknown Japan—of today.

These changes include more multilingual signs in strategic places, more information kiosks [designated by the International "I" sign, more foreign language speaking guides, more menus printed in English and other languages and a variety of other small but very helpful steps that take most of the mystery and uncertainty of getting around in Japan.

By all of the measures and standards of tourism that count, Japan ranks near the top of the list of the world's best travel destinations, and once this becomes known it will surely receive the recognition it deserves.

[2]
Japan's Appeal to Foreigners Exotic and Sensual

As noted in my book *EXOTIC JAPAN* there are two Japans—the modern or Westernized Japan, and the traditional Japan. It is often said that it is the Western side of Japan that make it a comfortable place to visit. But it is the traditional elements that make it fascinating to the foreign visitor, and one of the world's best travel destinations.

The fascination that Japan holds for foreigners derives not only from the charm of the unfamiliar, but also from the fact that so many facets of traditional Japan are striking, intriguing, unusual, beautiful, and the very essence of exotic to foreign eyes.

What makes Japan even more interesting to the foreign visitor is that one can move freely and effortlessly back and forth between the modern and traditional, as easily and as quickly as passing through a door. In fact, a door is often the only dividing line between the two worlds.

And not surprising to those who are familiar with Oriental cultures, there is a strong sensual element in the exotic side of Japan—from its traditional architecture, arts, crafts and wearing apparel to the extraordinary number and variety of festivals and other customs that make up the essence and flavor of Japanese culture.

What makes the impact of the traditional side of Japan so powerful is that the exotic and the sensual are combined. Both are integral elements of virtually everything that is culturally Japanese.

One might say that the Kanamara Festival of the Wakamiya Hachiman Shrine in Kawasaki City, between Tokyo and Yokohama, and the Honen Festival of the Tagata

Shrine in Komaki City, are two of the extremes of the sensual side of Japanese culture.

These annual events, sometimes referred to as "fertility festivals," are built around activities involving replicas of the male phallus that range from small to eight feet or more in length. Young women ride phallus-shaped seesaws and eat phallus-shaped candies. Men, women and children get their pictures taken embracing huge phallic reproductions.

The sensual element in the kimono, the yukata, the paper doors and partitions in traditional homes and inns, the kitchen utensils, the wall decorations, the gardens—again in virtually everything that is Japanese—is far more subtle than the phallic festivals, but equally powerful over a period of time.

To Western eyes, few things are more exotic than Japan's kabuki and noh theatrical forms. And while not as overtly conspicuous, virtually everything else that is traditional in Japanese life also qualifies as exotic, from the ideograms used to write the language to the vast array of items one sees in department store food malls.

Another facet in the combination of the exotic and sensual in Japanese culture that attracts foreign visitors, especially Westerners, is the element of mystery. No matter how long foreigners stay in Japan, or how familiar they become with the people and the culture, the mystery remains.

This mystery persists because there are so many facets of Japanese culture that do not lend themselves to ready explanation, that remain beguiling and intriguing. Part of this perception may be attributed to the overblown "mystery of the Orient" image that has prevailed in the West for centuries, but most of it derives from elements of Japan's traditional culture that are demonstrated in the arts and crafts as well as in household furnishings and utensils…in the essence of things that make them *Japanese*.

In other words, a certain "Japanese sense" that is both conscious and unconscious is responsible for the exotic and erotic aspects of Japanese culture that foreigners find so appealing and so satisfying. This "sense" is automatically applied to virtually everything the Japanese do, from such mundane actions as preparing and arranging food on a plate to landscaping a Zen garden or conducting a tea ceremony.

The visitor who wants to get the most out of Japan should be prepared to look beyond the Western facade that obscures the essence and heart of the traditional culture, for that is where the pleasure—and benefit—resides.

[3]
More Secrets of Japan's Appeal to Westerners

WHEN THE FIRST Westerners of record stumbled onto Japan in the 1540s, the discovery of the islands by Europeans resulted in an influx of traders and Christian missionaries. Both of these groups were intent on expanding their empires in Asia.

Among the many things that astounded these first Western visitors to Japan was the incredible quality of its handicrafts and arts, and the ability of Japanese craftsmen to copy any Western product not only perfectly but to improve on it in the process.

Thereafter, Japanese arts and crafts as well as Western products made in Japan were shipped to Europe in large volume.

One of the extraordinary historical stories of this era: Japans now famous woodblock prints were so common and so cheap that they were used as wrapping paper on some of the goods shipped to Europe, where they became highly valued collectors items and had a fundamental influence on European artists of the period.

But the number of Europeans in Japan, and their influence, grew so rapidly that the Tokugawa Shogunate began to fear the country might be colonized by the Western powers. This fear resulted in a decision by the Shogunate in the 1630s to expel all foreigners from the country except for a small detachment of Dutch traders, who were kept confined on a small man-made islet in Nagasaki Bay, and to ban all travel from and to the country.

For the next 200-plus years this tiny Dutch trading post and occasional officially approved visits by Chinese and

Korean ships were Japan's only contacts with the outside world.

Japan's isolation from the Western world did not end until the early 1850s, when the United States sent a fleet of warships into Tokyo Bay in 1853 and demanded that Japan open its doors to trade and diplomatic intercourse.

Powerless in the face of the American warships, and aiming to control the situation as much as possible, the Shogunate agreed to the American demand, and in March of 1854 signed a pact opening two ports to American ships and agreeing to accept a diplomatic representative. Soon thereafter similar pacts were signed with England, Russia and the Netherlands.

During the next decade, foreign traders and missionaries flocked to Japan, this time with Americans leading the charge. But the signing of the pacts by the Shogunate in Edo (Tokyo) outraged some of the outlying provincial lords in the southwest. They began agitating for the return of the Emperor (in Kyoto) to power.

This agitation led to a civil war in the mid-1860s, resulting in the downfall of the Shogunate in 1867 and the restoration of the Emperor who had not exercised real authority since 1185.

The Japanese were fascinated by Western products, and began to disparage their own arts and crafts. Western importers once again began taking advantage of the Japanese ability to copy products, and by 1900 products made in Japan were flooding Western markets, earning the Japanese the reputation of being nothing but copiers and makers of cheap goods.

It was not until the early 1960s that Japan's manufacturers were able to get out from under the control of foreign buyers and bring their traditional standards of quality into the production of Western style products. And as the saying goes, the rest is history.

What was the source of Japan's traditional quality standards? How were the Japanese able to raise the quality standards of their handicrafts to that of a fine art? This too, relates to their skill in copying and improving upon things they copy, but in this case it goes back more than a thousand years.

Beginning around 300 A.D. Chinese ideas and products began trickling into Japan, mostly through Korea and via Korean immigrants to the islands. Over the next 500 years, virtually all of these imported products, now regarded as Japanese, became the foundation of the economy and the culture of Japan.

Along with these products came the ancient Chinese custom of the master-apprentice approach to the arts and crafts. But the Japanese didn't just imitate the Chinese and Koreans. They institutionalized and ritualized the master-apprentice training methods, adding to it the concept of *kaizen* (kigh-zen) or continuous improvement.

As the generations passed, these institutions and rituals were strengthened by the introduction of the Zen principles of dispensing with the superfluous and harmonizing life and nature, resulting in masters who could actually achieve virtual perfection in the arts and crafts.

This was the Japan that Westerners first encountered in the 1500s and again in the 1800s, by which time, the Japanese were so conditioned in the principles and practices of quality that they didn't think about it, and achieving it was simply the Japanese way of doing things.

Another important factor that distinguishes traditional Japanese arts and crafts, as well as many of its modern products, is a look and a feel that is unique, that grows out of the psychic of the Japanese that precedes their contact with Korea and China.

The influence of this "Japanese thing" on Westerners varies from very weak to very strong, depending on their sensitivity and aesthetic development. But it influences everyone to some degree. To the sensitive person, it has a calming, soothing effect on the intellect and the spirit, and creates a harmonious repose with nature.

Westerners who visit Japan, even for a few days, are invariably touched by this unique facet of Japanese culture.

[4]
The Aesthetic Side of Japanese Culture Has Powerful Influence

ONE OF THE the most remarkable things about Japan's traditional lifestyle was the role that the appreciation of beauty played in the daily lives of the people. It seems that the Japanese were among the few people known to history to have made aesthetics an integral part of their culture.

The origin of this extraordinary phenomenon, which was universal, applying to the high and the low alike, can be found in Shinto, the indigenous religion of the Japanese, and in Taoism and Buddhism, the latter two imported from China between 400 and 600 A.D.

In Shinto, nature is the handiwork of the gods. Recognizing and celebrating the beauty of nature is therefore a way of respecting and honoring both nature and its divine creators.

Lao Tsu, the founder of Taoism (The Way), taught that there was beauty in everything in nature, and that it was up to the viewer to see it. The great Tao masters who followed Lao Tsu further taught that it was possible to fully appreciate beauty only if a person allowed beauty to permeate his being and direct his life.

Buddhism recognized the beauty and harmony in nature, and advocated that people pattern their lives on the natural order of things, attempting to achieve both harmony and beauty in their daily lives.

The combination of these influences eventually permeated Japanese culture, becoming the guidelines and standards for the arts and crafts, for all of the artifacts and implements the Japanese used in their daily life, and for many of the recreational and cultural customs that developed over the generations, from flower-viewing to sightseeing.

These influences eventually culminated in the country's famous "tea ceremony," which is an exercise in pure aestheticism….rather than an occasion for drinking tea.

The nature of beauty as defined by the greatest tea masters is Summed up in the word *shibumi* (she-buu-me), which can be translated as astringent, simple, conservative, unaffected, elegant, etc.

Shibui (she-booey) beauty is beauty that is in perfect harmony with nature and has a tranquil affect on the viewer. It imparts serenity, nobility and quiet luxury. It is a work of art in which all of the elements are harmoniously arranged and balanced.

After centuries of exposure to the principles and practices of *shibui* living the Japanese developed the ability to recognize and produce this quality almost instinctively. They did not have to strain to judge whether or not something was beautiful, or to create it.

It is the *shibui* quality in Japanese things that make them *Japanese*; that gives them an aura that is sensual and pleasing to the eye and to the touch. And it is the *shibui* aspects of Japan—from its architecture, arts, crafts, and interior decoration to how food is arranged on a tray— along with the character and behavior of the people, that foreign visitors find so appealing.

This *shibui* effect is visceral and sensual, and affects everyone, including those who are not consciously aware of its influence. It clearly explains why so many foreigners in the past chose to live in Japan despite many inconveniences and a long list of things they loved to complain about.

Virtually all of those old inconveniences and other reasons for complaining have disappeared, and while the traditional *shibui* side of life in Japan is often overshadowed by modern things, it is still there in abundance, providing an exotic and erotic flavor to life that continues to work its magic.

But experiencing this traditional side of Japan must be planned and done deliberately. Short-term visitors in particular should make a number of informed choices on what they want to see and do while in Japan, and plan their trip accordingly.

A few of the obvious things: spending at least one night in a Japanese style inn (*ryokan* / rio-kahn); dining in several Japanese style restaurants where patrons sit on *tatami* (tah-tah-me) reed-mat floors; spending at least one night in an *onsen* (own-sen) hot springs resort inn; attend and participate in a tea ceremony; go to a Zen Buddhist temple for a *zazen* (zah-zen) or seated meditation session; and watch a couple of *chambara* (chahm-bah-rah) movies—those set in Shogunate times and featuring samurai warriors and townsfolk. [They are the Japanese version of American Westerns and such sword-fighting films as the tale of Robin Hood, and pirate stories.]

[5]
Japan's Amazing Traditions Of Recreational Travel

JAPAN WAS ONE of the first, if not the first, country in the world in which recreational travel by large numbers of people became a full-fledged industry.

The Japanese urge to travel for enjoyment has been a significant part of the culture since ancient times, and may have had its genesis in the incredible beauty of the islands and in the development of an extraordinary aesthetic sense in the Japanese psyche.

The mythological gods credited with creating the Japanese islands were so impressed with their handiwork that they descended from the heavens to take up permanent residence on the islands.

Poetry written well over a thousand years ago extols the beauty of the islands, and makes it evident that the writers had traveled. Buddhism and Shintoism also played a key role in travel in ancient Japan, as monks and priests sought out locations of exceptional beauty in distant mountains to build temples and shrines that attracted visitors from afar.

During the golden Heian era (A.D. 794-1185) traveling for recreational purposes was especially common among the elite, and over the centuries, hundreds of places around the islands became famous for their exceptional beauty.

But it was not until founding of the Tokugawa Shogunate in 1603 and the beginning of over two centuries of peace and prosperity that the average Japanese were able to travel for recreational and for religious purposes

In 1635 the Shogunate mandated a political control system that required over 260 of the country's some 300 fief lords to keep their families in Edo at all times, and themselves, along with a large entourage of retainers, spend every other year in Edo.

This resulted in the construction of a network of inns, a day's march apart, on the five great roads leading to Edo from the rest of the country. While built to accommodate the domain lords and their entourages, the inns catered to other travelers as well.

As the decades passed, the roads and inns became crowded with religious pilgrims, gamblers, salesmen, sumo wrestlers, roving monks and priests, government officials, messengers, painters, poets, and secret agents.

Two types of travel became institutionalized in Japanese life: *monomode* (moh-no-moh-day), which consisted of walking tours of famous shrines and temples around the country (that often lasted for months); and *yusan* (yuu-sahn), which were sightseeing trips to famous scenic places (numbering in the hundreds).

With a nod to the scriptwriters of the Bob Hope and Bing Crosby "road movies," the first such "road" stories were written by Ikku Jippensha between 1802 and 1822. These stories were entitled *Tokaido Chu Hizakurige*, which translates as "Traveling the East Sea Road by Shank's Mare" (on foot).

The series of books chronicled the adventures of two men from Edo, Yajirobe and Kitahachi, who preferred the pleasures and perils of the road to the carping of their wives.

The two dyed-in-the-wool Edo-type men (boisterous, argumentative, and proud) got into every type of comic situation imaginable, and in the process of telling their stories, the author provides a vivid account of the manners and morals of Japanese life during that era in Japan's history.

The emergence of modern Japan gave rise to three other great categories of domestic travelers—hordes of school children on excursions that were mandated by the Ministry of Education in the late 1800s, millions of big city residents returning to their ancestral villages and towns on holidays and other occasions, and huge numbers of business people going to and fro, from the northernmost island of Hokkaido to the southern island of Okinawa.

In the 1950s, villages and rural organizations nationwide renewed the custom of sponsoring group trips to major cities and scenic attractions. By the mid-1950s virtually all companies in Japan were sponsoring annual outings for their employees to beaches, hot spring spas or mountain retreats.

Today, virtually all Japanese make at least one overnight trip away from their homes and offices each year, and millions travel within the country from a few to dozens of times every year.

[6]
Japan's Shoguns Created The World's First Travel Industry

IT MAY BE something of a surprise to most people that the travel industry as it is known today originated in Japan. As already noted, Japan was the first country in the world to have a nationwide network of roadside inns, and the first country in the world in which great numbers of ordinary people routinely traveled long distances on pleasure trips.

All of this came about because of the Tokugawa Shogunate policy, known as *Sankin Kotai* (Sahn-keen Koh-tie), or "Alternate Attendance," that required that the leaders of fiefs throughout the country to keep their families in Edo at all times as hostages, and the fief lords themselves spend every other year in Edo in attendance at the Shogun's Court—a clever ploy designed to help prevent them from becoming a threat to the new government.

This decree specified how many retainers—samurai warriors, aides and servants -- the *Daimyo* (Dime-yoh) or fief lords were required to bring with them to Edo on their semi-annual trips, based on the income of their fiefs—a strategy designed to cost them as much as 70 percent of their income and keep in them economically and militarily weak.

The trips of the lords and their entourages to and from Edo came to be known as *Daimyo Gyoretsu* (Dime-yoh G'yoh-rate-sue) or "Processions of the Lords." The typical entourage ranged from 150 to 350 people. The richest of the lords, Maeda, was required to bring up to a thousand retainers with him.

The *Sankin Kotai* decree also designated which roads the fief lords would travel from and to their domains, and required that towns and villages along the various routes construct and staff suitable accommodations for the *Daimyo* and their retainers at intervals of one day's march. Local residents were also required to maintain the roads in their vicinity and plant trees along them.

In 1637, Ieyasu's grandson, Iemitsu, the third Tokugawa Shogun, dramatically expanded the scope of the *Sankin Kotai* system to cover over 260 of the some 300 fief lords in the country, making it one of the defining characteristics of the nation's economy and social life.

The expansion of this extraordinary system of political and economic control required a major construction program that resulted in the already existing network of inns being extended throughout the main islands.

The Shogunate decree mandated three classes of inns:

Honjin (Hone-jeen), which can be translated as "Head Inns." These inns, richly appointed in the style of the imperial mansions of Kyoto, were reserved for the lords and their personal aides.

Waki Honjin (Wah-kee Hone-jeen) or "Annex Head Inns." These inns were only slightly less luxurious then the *Honjin* and were reserved for other ranking guests when the *Honjin* were full.

Hatago (Hah-tah-go), which were the equivalent of today's Holiday Inns, and were reserved for the lord's warriors and lower ranking staff and servants.

On just one road, the *Tokaido* (Toh-kigh-doh) or East Sea Road, which connected Kyoto to Edo, there were 93 Honjin, 102 Waki Honjin, and 1,812 Hatago inns. There were four other great roads leading to Edo that were also lined with inns.

Not only did the *Sankin Kotai* system result in the development of a highly sophisticated network of inns nationwide, it was also responsible for the development of the traditions of extraordinary service that are still characteristic of Japanese hotels and inns, and for the spread of a refined level of culture throughout the rural areas of Japan.

These truly remarkable "Processions of the Lords" continued to be a defining characteristic of Japanese life for more than 200 years, not ending until 1862.

Each year this long custom is reprised along the shores of Lake Hakone where the most important roadway barrier was maintained during the Tokugawa era. The event, held on November 3, Culture Day, is a major attractive for Japanese as well as visitors from abroad.

The authentically costumed participants in the procession march from the town of Yumoto Hot Springs to Hakone.

[7]
The Amazing Traditions Of Goodwill & Service

LAFCADIO Hearn, a Greek-island born writer (the son of an Anglo father and a Greek mother) who arrived in Japan in the 1890s on assignment for an American magazine, became entranced with the attitudes and behavior of the common people, and wrote that life in Japan was like living in paradise.

There were many who disputed this idealistic view of Japan, but Hearn was, in fact, on to something.

For more than a thousand years before Hearn's arrival in Tokyo, the foundation for Japan's culture had been *wa* (wah) or harmony, based on a concept known as *amae* (ah-my), which may be translated as "indulgent love."

In essence, *amae* referred to treating people with the utmost respect and propriety, never doing anything to upset others, and going out of your way to be kind, thoughtful and generous.

Obviously this philosophy did not prevent all aggression and violence in Japanese society, particularly among the ruling class, but it did permeate the attitudes and behavior of the common people to a degree that is rare in human history.

The ordinary people of Japan were law-abiding, honest and thoughtful to a degree that was astounding to visitors from the West, and despite all of the changes in Japan since the end of the 19th century, enough of this traditional cultural remains in Japanese society to set them apart from most other people.

Bicycles, store merchandise—you name it—are left on sidewalks and streets without fear that they will be stolen.

Taxi drivers turn in anything left in their cabs! Individuals go to extreme lengths to return wallets found on streets or in other areas, with the contents intact!

Japan's traditional culture also made hospitality a moral and philosophical facet of their character, particularly in their behavior toward guests and seniors, a phenomenon that grew out of their native religion, Shinto, and the influence of Buddhism and other concepts and customs imported from China.

And what was equally impressive to Hearn—and millions of people who have since visited Japan—was, and is, the level of service that is an integral part of the lives of the people—in every facet of their lives, from the manufacturing and wholesaling industries to the retail trades.

And nowhere are these traditions of service more obvious, and more impressive, than in the inn, hotel, restaurant and nighttime entertainment industries.

As in the case of so many aspects of Japanese culture, this extra-ordinary standard of service rose to the level of an art during the Tokugawa Shogunate era (1603-1867)—a phenomenon that grew out of the fact that the standards of etiquette and service in the Shogun's Court and in the courts of the 300 provincial lords was spread throughout the country.

There are a great many things in Japan today that are impressive to visitors, but when it comes down to what really makes the most lasting and the most positive impression on visitors from abroad is the character of the people—their attitudes and behavior toward others in general, and especially toward customers and guests.

The traditional etiquette of the Japanese—how they behaved toward each other in both social and business settings—was based on the highly refined and stylized manners that developed in the Imperial Court in Kyoto and, like their concept of service, spread from there to the courts of the shoguns and provincial lords, then to samurai families, and finally to the whole of society.

An old story dramatically illustrates the level of Japan's traditional etiquette. In the 1890s a London banker became a devotee of the Japanese tea ceremony and told his counterpart in Tokyo that he would like to have a teahouse built on his property.

The Tokyo banker dispatched a carpenter to London to build the house. The London banker was so impressed with the manners of the carpenter that he mistook him for a member of Japan's upper class, and greeted him accordingly. He was astounded to discover that the man was a common worker.

[8]
Honored Guest Syndrome Makes Japanese Great Hosts

THERE IS a tradition of hospitality in the Orient that flies in the face of the historical circumstances of the vast majority of the people of Asia. From the dawn of their history until recent times, some 90 percent of all Asians lived at, or only slightly above, bare survival levels.

And it seems that in those countries in which the economies provided the least in the way of food and other amenities, the traditions of hospitality to guests and strangers were the strongest.

Mongolians, whose lifestyle on the bare, wind-swept plains of central Asia was always rigorous and frequently life-threatening, have traditionally been among the most hospitable of all people and today they remain famous for readily and happily sharing what they have with visitors.

In countries that are in the Buddhist sphere of Asia, the poor and the affluent alike were taught that generosity and giving was both a religious duty and a way of building up divine merit—and much of this legacy remains today.

From the dawn of their own history, the Japanese were first influenced to believe in and practice hospitality by Shintoism, their indigenous religion, and by their subsistence-level lifestyle, and then for the last a millennium and a half, by the doctrines of Buddhism.

There were other immediate factors that helped make hospitality to guests a key part of the Japanese lifestyle and mindset. These factors, based on customs first practiced in the Imperial Court in Kyoto, then in the Court of the Shoguns in Edo (Tokyo) and finally in the Courts of the fief lords, included highly stylized ways of welcoming, seating and treating guests with special care that, over the centuries, became deeply embedded in the culture.

But there appears to be another element in the Japanese view and practice of hospitality toward visitors, Westerners in particular. This element, which they share with both Koreans the Chinese, seems to derive from pride in their race and in their country—a pride that typically compels them to go above and beyond a degree of hospitality that would be more than sufficient.

The desire and efforts of the typical Japanese to make a good impression on visitors is sincere, and their enthusiasm to do so often seems to be unbounded. Japanese contacts and friends—sometimes even strangers—will often pay restaurant and transportation bills when by all rights it should be the foreign side that pays.

When these situations occur and the foreigner protests, the Japanese will say such things as "When you are in Japan you are our guest."

The legacy of all these influences to extend hospitality to guests remains strong in Japan, and when it is combined with the traditional Japanese commitment to service, which borders on a social if not a cultural imperative, it becomes a valuable asset, not only for the travel industry but for the country as a whole.

Japan's combination of hospitality and service was honed to virtual perfection during the last Shogunate era (Tokugawa, 1603-1867), and is especially conspicuous today in the hotel, inn and restaurant industries—areas that are on the frontline of tourism.

Leaders in Japan's tourism industry have recently experienced a kind of epiphany insofar as the value of the hospitality and service traditions are concerned. Recognizing that these cultural attitudes and practices need to be taught to each new generation, they are encouraging new and more comprehensive training of industry employees.

Hotels, inns and restaurants that have successfully instituted training programs based on traditional attitudes and behavior stand out the moment one enters. The more this "return to the past" is emphasized, the more successful Japan's tourism industry is likely to be in the future.

Many of Japan's major hotels stage a number of events each year that duplicate authentic slices of life from the past—from sumo demonstrations of pounding cooked rice into glutinous rice to bake omochi cakes for New Year's, to demonstrations by artists and craftsmen.

[9]
Special Amenities Come With Life in Japan

THERE ARE many aspects of life in Japan that come under the category of *yuga* (yuuh-gah), a word that means "graceful" as well as "elegant" and refers to those things that make life in Japan especially satisfying—physically, emotionally, intellectually and spiritually. [Anything that can touch all of these bases in the human experience should have a high priority in all societies!]

Among the tangible factors in Japanese life that are high on the list of *yuga* things are *O'shibori* (Oh-she-boh-ree). An *O'shibori* is a small hand-towel—heated in the winter and cooled in the summer—that is handed out to customers in Japanese style restaurants, inns, bars, clubs, etc.

There are few things as refreshing as wiping one's face and hands with an *O'shibori* on a cold day or a sweltering, hot day, and once you have experienced the custom the memory of it stays with you for life.

Some places enhance the sensual pleasure provided by their *O'shibori* by adding an aroma to the water they are soaked in. One of the most pleasing and refreshing of these aromas is the essence of jasmine.

O'shibori are big business in Japan. Suppliers of the towels and the compact appliances used for cooling and heating abound throughout the country. You can also buy packaged *O'shibori* in stores.

Some foreign airlines serving Japan have made a small gesture toward the *O'shibori* custom. They pass out tiny pieces of wet paper that have been impregnated with a pleasant smell. They leave a lot to be desired!

Hot spring spas are another of the amenities of life in Japan that, while not unique, are far more ubiquitous than in any other country. Altogether there are over 2,000 hot spring spas in the country—many of them mineral springs that are efficacious for a variety of ailments. Individual spas have from three or four to over 700 inns. Each inn has one or more hot spring baths.

That's a lot of hot water, and the spas attract several million bathers each year, providing a sensual experience that is especially pleasing to the body and the mind.

Another of the Japanese amenities that foreign visitors appreciate are the *yukata* (yuu-kah-tah) robes that are provided by hotels and inns for their guests. The lightweight, colorful robes are not just bathrobes. They are also casual wear for both inside and outside use.

One of the special pleasures of staying in Japan's resort hotels and inns, particularly those in popular vacation spots, is strolling around in the shopping and entertainment districts in the late afternoon and evening dressed in a *yukata*.

All of the participants in many of Japan's annual festivals wear *yukata* as the formal, official costume. In cities and towns throughout the country, family members often don *yukata* after their evening bath, and attend summer festivities held by their neighborhood shrines and temples.

Food stalls on the streets are another of the attractions of life in Japan. Among the most popular of these stalls in the wintertime are those selling baked sweet potatoes and chestnuts. The stalls can generally be found in shopping areas, in parks, and near train stations.

In some neighborhoods still today, baked sweet potato vendors push their wheeled stalls up and down the streets, calling out *Yaki imo!* (yah-kee ee-moh!), "Baked sweet potatoes!," in a sing-song voice that stirs nostalgic memories in old-timers.

[The most nostalgic of these traditional customs has to be the tofu men who made their morning rounds, blowing on distinctive horns to alert housewives to their early morning presence. In Tokyo, at least, they seem to have gone by the wayside.]

On special occasions, some of Japan's hotels have food stalls set up in their lobby areas, offering guests and visitors a special treat.

Another amenity that goes with life in Japan is free food samples passed out by vendors in department stores. Department stores in Japan generally have a large army of "prepared food" vendors in their first and sometimes second basement floors, many of which offer feature free food samples.

In many of these stores, shoppers can start out with an appetizer, test the ingredients of a main dish, like fish or steak, and then finish off with a dessert.

Among other "amenities" that come with living in Japan are free packets of tissue paper that are passed out at train stations by companies of all kinds as part of their advertising. According to published statistics, over two billion of these little packets are passed out each year.

They not only come in handy, they make nice little token gifts to take home and give to friends.

Perhaps the most powerful of all of the "amenities" that make Japan a unique place for Western residents and visitors is the exotic quality of all things Japanese, from the traditional arts, crafts, and interior decorations to the food.

[10]
Getting the Feel of the Real Japan!

DESPITE ALL OF the amazing artifacts of Japan—historical and modern—and despite the sublime beauty of its mountains and coast-lines, the real attraction of the island country is the Japanese themselves.

In fact, people who come to Japan and limit their sight-seeing to its historical grandeurs and its modern-day façade of high-rise buildings, amazing "bullet trains," bridges and tunnels that connect islands, shops that make Rodeo Drive in Los Angeles look dowdy, and more, are short-changing themselves.

One of the keys to getting a real feel for Japan, and thereby getting the most out of a visit, is to rub elbows (and other parts of the anatomy) with the people themselves, and simply to "people-watch"—viewing huge numbers of them, in public, as they go to and fro.

There are literally several thousand outstanding people-watching locations in Tokyo alone. To make things easier for visitors, I have selected several spots, each of which has a personality of its own, that would most likely be regarded as at least in the top twenty locations in the city by most experienced people-watchers.

Three of these locations are within a short walk of each other. They are the main Ginza Intersection where Hibiya and Chuo Streets intersect at Ginza 4-chome; the Sukiyabashi Intersection, about 200 yards west of the Ginza Intersection, where Hibiya Street intersects with Sotobori Street; and the Hibiya theater and restaurant district another 200 yards or further west, adjoining Hibiya

Street on the south side—very near the Imperial Hotel and the Peninsula Hotel.

Since the late 1800s, most Tokyo residents have considered the Ginza 4-chome intersection as the unofficial the center of the city. Its famous Mitsukoshi and Wako Department Stores are historical icons.

For really old-timers, the Mitsukoshi Department Store building on the NE corner of the intersection was the main Post Exchange for the U.S, military during the 1945-1952 occupation of Japan, and there was a U.S. run hamburger and milk shake cafeteria in the basement of the Wako Department Store building on the NW corner of the intersection.

The Sukiyabashi Intersection, just a few blocks away, is probably the most filmed, and therefore internationally the most familiar, intersection in Japan…the special attraction being the amazing display of nighttime neon signs on the NE corner. Sony's main product display building is on the SE corner of the intersection, and the Hankyu Department Store is on the SW corner.

The nearby Hibiya district is the location of the Tokyo branch of the famous Takarazuka Theater, which features all-female revues on the scale seen in Paris and Las Vegas, along with several other theaters and food courts in the basements of adjoining office buildings, as well a number of narrow restaurant alleys.

The Roppongi district, a few subway minutes from the Ginza/Hibiya areas, is a maze of narrow streets that are home to hundreds of bars, nightclubs and restaurants that run the gamut from plush to dives. The district is a major draw for foreign residents, film stars, fashion models and others wanting to make some kind of statement.

Shibuya, a few minutes further on in a southwesterly direction (on the Yamanote commuter Loop Line that encircles central Tokyo), might be called "young town," as it is a night-time and weekend mecca for young people, drawn to the area as a meeting place (at Hachiko, "the dog" in Shibuya Plaza in front of Shibuya Station), and for its plethora of apparel and accessory shops, restaurants, bars, bookstores, record stores, etc.

Then moving one station to the north on the Yamanote commuter train line we have the Harajuku district and Omotesando Boulevard, which now competes with Chuo Ave-nue [the main Ginza thoroughfare] as the city's most popular strolling street.

In addition to the upscale fashion shops and restaurants fronting on Omotesando, the district's maze of side streets are chocked full of shops carrying the kind of far-out clothing favored by the far-out young. In fact, it is the dress, make-up and behavior of the thousands of young people who flock to Harajuku on holidays and the weekends that attracts hordes of sightseers.

Next on our list is Shinjuku, the second station going NW from Harajuku, with its department stores, office buildings, hotels, and notorious Kabukicho entertainment and restaurant district, a short walk from Shinjuku Station. Often described as sleazy and dangerous because many of its establishments are run by gangs (domestic and foreign), it is generally as safe as Sunday School, and draws huge numbers of people who are attracted by its reputation and what it has to offer.

One could easily add such well-known locations as Akasaka, Aoyama, Asakusa, and go on down the alphabetical line, all with their own special appeal, but the few noted should be enough to satiate the most avid people-watchers.

[11]
In Japan it's Not All Raw Fish, Rice & Noodles!

IF TYPICAL Westerners in advanced countries are asked to name their most important concerns regarding any foreign trip they might take, food is almost always high on their list.

Americans who have not traveled abroad before can be especially skittish about both food and water—in part because of [true] stories about visitors coming down with the "tourist trot" in countries where sanitary standards are low or virtually non-existent.

Those who are not familiar with Japan might assume that sanitation standards there may also be low, and that special care must be taken to avoid being exposed to unfriendly bacteria. There is no need for such concern.

As it happens, the Japanese were among the first, if not the first, people to develop extraordinarily high standards of sanitation in all areas of their lives…something they owe to their native religion, Shinto.

One of the primary tenets of Shinto is that cleanliness is an aspect of godliness, resulting in the Japanese being acutely concerned about cleanliness from the dawn of their history, and developing a lifestyle in which cleanliness was a moral value that became deeply engrained in their lifestyle.

Long before Westerners ever equated bathing with good health and the advantages of keeping their homes and workplaces clean, the Japanese scrubbed themselves daily in hot water, then soaked in hot tubs as an added health measure. [When the first Westerners showed up in Japan, their body odor was such that the Japanese could not stand to be near them.]

The Japanese also cleaned their homes daily. Cooking and eating utensils were washed after each use. People not only cleaned themselves and their houses daily, they also kept the area around their homes scrupulously clean.

This virtual obsession with cleanliness has remained a key element in Japanese culture, and still today is one of the reasons why foreign visitors are so impressed with the people and the country. Visitors do not have to be concerned about the sanitation standards in Japanese restaurants, or anywhere else for that matter, including at street vendor stalls.

This is good news, of course, but it is only half of the news where food and dining out are concerned. When it comes to food and restaurants, Japan is one of the most cosmopolitan and international countries in the world.

All of the major cuisines of the world—American, British, Chinese, French, German, Greek, Italian, Mexican, Russian, etc.—are available in Japan, in common, middle and upscale restaurants. Regional and local cuisines, from Indian, Indonesian, Korean, Malaysian and Thai to Tibetan are also available.

The number of "Japanese" restaurants that serve a variety of chicken, fish, meat and vegetable dishes that are Western in both appearance and taste is astounding. Western chain restaurants, particularly the fast food variety, are cheek-by-jowl in every city in the country.

Japanese restaurants serving traditional dishes, from sushi and noodles to combinations of rice, chicken, beef, eggs, pork and seafood—all of which, with the possible exception of raw fish, most Westerners like the very first time they try them—also abound throughout the country.

Office buildings typically have half a dozen or so restaurants in their basements. Newer, larger buildings have as many as fifty or sixty restaurants in their basements and on upper floors devoted entirely to upscale eateries, many of which offer panoramic views of the surrounding areas.

All of Japan's major cities have what amounts to "restaurant districts" made up of dozens to hundreds of restaurants that attract diners as well as casual strollers who enjoy the sights, sounds and exotic ambiance.

Obviously, the Japanese are great diner outers…they have to be to support the incredible number and variety of restaurants—there are well over 800,000 restaurants in the small county—and they do so with a sense of adventure. They flock to new restaurants that offer anything new in the way of style or food.

First-time visitors to Japan should also make a point of having as many food experiences as possible. In addition to adding to their culinary knowledge and pleasuring the palate, it makes it possible for them to "rub elbows" with the Japanese and share in their daily life—one of the main benefits of visiting the country.

Coffee shops in international hotels are far less expensive than the specialty restaurants in the hotels, but they are typically more expensive than the same dishes sold by restaurants outside of the hotels—and in virtually all cases there are a few to dozens of restaurants with short walks of the top hotels—not to mention really inexpensive shops surrounding all commuter train stations as well as food kiosks on long-distance station platforms.

There are up to 50 or more restaurants in some train station buildings and in adjoining buildings. These restaurant malls invariably include branches of many of the most famous and popular restaurants in the country.

[12]
Restaurants in Japan
Epitome of Good Taste

JAPAN'S TRADITIONAL culture programmed the aesthetic sense of the people to an extraordinary degree, imbuing them with a sense of design that was well above the ordinary, and making them design and quality critics of a very high order.

This aesthetic programming was built into the culture by the constant striving of all artists and craftsmen to achieve perfection in their work, the influence of leaning how to draw the complicated characters or ideograms making up the writing system, and a number of deeply entrenched customs for appreciating beauty and functionality in all of the mundane artifacts of their lives as well as their daily behavior.

The design heritage of the Japanese is now making itself felt worldwide, as more and more foreign designers pick up on the principles of Japanese design and integrate them into their own work.

And no where (naturally enough) are Japan's traditions of good design more conspicuous than in Japan itself. One area of good design that is especially notable is the restaurant business.

There are some 800,000 restaurants in Japan, attesting to the fact that eating out is one of the most popular customs in the country. These restaurants range from tiny "holes in the wall" to swanky dinner clubs that cater to the rich and famous.

But what is of special interest is the quality of the design in what can be described as ordinary restaurants that cater to the hoi polloi. The furnishings and interior décoration of many of them are awesome in both an aesthetic and functionality sense.

What makes this even more remarkable is that most of these restaurants were not designed and decorated by professional designers. They were created by ordinary people.

The foreign visitor who dines out in Japan and does not take notice of the design quality of so many restaurants, particularly those that serve traditional Japanese dishes, is missing one of the pleasures of being in the country.

Some choices in Tokyo: Soba Giro (in Prudential Plaza, Nagato-cho); Yamato (teppanyaki in the Mikasa Kaikan on the Ginza); the Hibiki chain (traditional dishes including zaru tofu, the Ginza, Marunouchi, Shidome, Odaiba, Shinjuku); Sakyo Higashiyama (Kyoto cuisine, the Ginza); Kuromoto (specializes in fugu, the poisonous globe fish, Aoyama).

Also Inakaya East and Inakaya West (both in Roppongi…Inakaya West is famous enough to attract visiting prime ministers, presidents and entertainment celebrities… Inakaya figuratively means "country food place").

Inakaya West is not cheap, but if you are putting on the dog for yourself or someone else, it is an impressive experience.

[13]
Fast Foods Invented In Japan Ages Ago

IT IS QUITE possible that "fast foods" were invented in Japan—and, of course, we're talking about Japanese style fast foods.

It seems that purveyors of fast foods first appeared in Japan before the beginning of recorded history in conjunction with neighborhood, district, regional and national Shinto shrines.

Large numbers of people visited these shrines to attend festivals and other special occasions, resulting in early day entrepreneurs setting up *yatai* (yah-tie), or portable food stalls, in the vicinity of the shrines as well as along the roads leading to the ones that were farther away.

As the generations passed and the population of Japan grew, the number of *yatai* at more popular shrines grew in proportion to the number of visitors, eventually numbering dozens on the shrine grounds and hundreds along the roads leading to the regional and national shrines.

Many of the shrines—there were well over 100,000 in the country—gradually gave birth to villages that morphed into towns, as other vendors took advantage of the ready-made shoppers by setting up stands and then shops and selling religious talismans and local handicrafts as souvenirs.

The success of the *yatai* at shrines led to their proliferation at other locations where crowds gathered, including sumo wrestling matches and cherry blossom viewing.

The adoption of Buddhism from China between the 5th and 7th centuries led to an amazing proliferation of temples throughout Japan, first because the Imperial Court ordered all landed estate managers to build temples in their provinces to promote the new religion, and second when individual Buddhist monks began to build their own temples.

This extraordinary phenomenon resulted in an equally impressive increase in the number of *yatai* in the country. The proliferation of courtesan districts during the Tokugawa shogunate era (1603-1868), also contributed to the number of *yatai*.

Despite the astounding number of restaurants that have appeared since the mid-1900s, the venerable *yatai* have survived into modern times. Today they can be found in all of the traditional places, as well as in parks, near bus and train stations, and on sidewalks in busy shopping districts.

Among the most popular fast foods sold by *yatai:* soba, udon, and ramen (all of which are noodle dishes in broth), oden, okonomi-yaki, monja-yaki, yaki-imo and kuri.

Oden (oh-dane) is a kind of stew that includes Japanese radish, fish cakes, eggs, tofu, onions, fried soybean curd, kelp, and konnyaku (a jelly made from a plant). It is cooked in a large flat-bed pan built into the top of the *yatai*, and is kept simmering hot.

Both okonomi-yaki (oh-koh-nomi-yah-kee) and monja-yaki (moan-jah-yha-kee) are flat pancake-like creations that contain such ingredients as egg, seafood (shrimp, squid, ocotopus, scallops), beef, pork, vegetables and corn. Monja-yaki is similar to okonomi-yaki, but is thinner and is sometimes referred to as "downtown okonomi-yaki."

Yaki-imo (Yah-kee ee-moh) are baked sweet potatoes, and kuri (kuu-ree) are roasted chestnuts. These two offerings, along with oden, are most popular during the cooler and colder months.

One also occasionally runs across a *yatai* selling *gyoza* (g'yoh-zah), the Chinese deep-fried garlic-laden crescent-shaped dumpling stuffed with ground pork.

Most oden-ya (oh-dane-yah) also stock and sell sake and beer, making them the pared down equivalent of an open-air snack and bar.

Yatai are one of the facets of Japan that add a special ambiance to the lifestyle, for visitors and residents alike.

In addition to the indigenous fast food restaurants in Japan KFC, McDonald's and other foreign food chains have had a major presence in Japan since the 1960s and 70s, so no one has to go without their fast-food fix.

[14]
Japan's Izakaya Out-Do Ireland's Pubs

IRELAND IS famous for its pubs. Japan should be even *more* famous for its *izakaya* (ee-zah-kah-yah).

Izakaya literally means "public drinking place," but they are more than just bars or lounges that serve drinks. They also serve food, and larger ones have extensive menus. They are also set apart from regular bars by their décor, their furniture, and the way the staff greets and serves customers.

When people in Japan go out to drink they may go to a bar or a lounge, where the décor is subdued and the atmosphere is quiet. But when they go out to party and to entertain guests, it is invariably understood that they go to an *izakaya*.

A spate of new books on the *izakaya* reveals just how widespread they are and the role they play in Japanese life. The books identify three categories of *izakaya*: those that evoke nostalgia for the past; those that are decades old and appeal to older people, and those with atmosphere that is thick with the intimacy of the traditional Japanese way of life, and inspires fiction writers.

For the record, government statistics show that there are approximately 150,000 *izakaya* in Japan, a remarkable number given fact that the urbanized area of the entire country is about the size of a single county in a larger American state. [In addition, there are some 198,000 bars, cabarets and nightclubs in Japan's cities, attesting again to the role that drinking plays in Japanese society.]

Seating in *izakaya* tends to be long, picnic-style wooden tables and benches. Staff members shout out greetings when patrons arrive and thanks when they leave in an atmosphere of raucous camaraderie that is not generally associated with the Japanese. Patrons typically share tables with strangers. Conversations are lively and loud.

Unlike other drinking establishments in Japan where most of the customers are male, *izakaya* patrons include couples, young women in twosomes and larger groups, and both young and middle-aged men. Many of the mixed-sex groups are co-workers.

Izakaya offer both foreign residents and visitors alike the best opportunity for experiencing a side of life in Japan that is far removed from the formality and rigidity of normal daytime activities, and far more revealing of the character of the Japanese.

Drinking alcoholic beverages has been an integral part of Japanese culture since its inception, first as a ritual associated with Shinto religious practices, then as a vital element in interpersonal relationships in both private and public settings, especially in business, political and other professional affairs.

Because drinking originated as a religious ritual it became imbued with deep-seated cultural meanings and uses that went well beyond the more casual approach to drinking alcoholic beverages that developed in the West.

To the Japanese, drinking was not just a recreational activity or an incidental way of relaxing and forgetting the cares of the day. It became the "oil" that lubricated relationships, the glue that bonded people, and the oath that formalized commitments and contracts.

Drinking also became the one culturally sanctified occasion when people could dispense with the strict etiquette that controlled their behavior and language at all other times—etiquette that made it critical for them to conduct themselves in the precise way prescribed for their social level, gender, and position.

It was only when drinking and having reached a certain level of intoxication that people could "let their hair down," speak relatively freely to each other, and behave in a rambunctious or licentious manner, depending on the venue and circumstances.

In earlier times there were probably more inns and restaurants in Japan that served alcoholic drinks than in any other country, with the possible exception of China.

Then in more modern times along came bars, cabarets and nightclubs in numbers that were astounding. And among these establishments, none were as important in the lives of ordinary people as the *izakaya*, the Japanese equivalent of the traditional Irish pubs and early American saloons and taverns.

If you are coming to Japan, I suggest that you put *izakaya* near the top of your list of things to do. [They remind me of the taverns that used to exist in the U.S.]

[15]
Beverage of the Gods Has Long History

VISITORS TO THE Nada area of Kobe, one of the earliest and most international of Japan's seaports, encounter an intriguing aroma that permeates the ground, the buildings, and the air.

This aroma is the scent of *O'sake* (Oh-sah-kay), Japan's original alcoholic beverage, which is still enshrined as the national drink. (The "O" in front of *sake* is an honorific.)

Sake, a kind of wine made from rice, has been brewed in Japan since shortly after the introduction of wet-rice farming in the third century B.C. and was the only alcoholic drink in the country until the introduction of European wines and whiskeys by foreign traders in the 16th century.

In early Japan, brewing and drinking *sake* was closely related to Shintoism. Every community shrine had its own rice paddies. At first, the rice from these fields was made into gruel, and eaten. Over a period of time, the process was refined to produce a clear liquid, and became drinkable.

The liquid version of *sake* was still considered a special offering to the gods, but as time passed it became common to drink it at parties and banquets not associated with shrine rituals. The Imperial Household has its own rice fields and *sake* brewery, as did temples and other institutions of the day.

To make *sake*, the rice is milled, washed, soaked and steamed. Then fresh spring water and yeast made from malted rice are added to induce fermentation. During the fermentation process, which lasts for about 20 days, the mixture seems to come alive, bubbling and making all kinds of sounds.

After fermentation, the wine is separated from the rice residue by running it through a press. The liquid is then filtered and placed in large vats, where it settles and becomes clear. It is then pasteurized and bottled. The alcoholic content of *sake* take from the top of the vat is from 12 to 14 percent. That taken from the lower turbid portion has an alcoholic content of 17 to 18 percent.

Sake is graded by a national inspection agency on the basis of taste, color and aroma, and comes in three grades: *tokkyu* (toke-que) or first grade; *ikkyu* (eek-que), second grade; and *nikkyu* (neek-que), third grade. The inspectors look for a subtle blend of sweetness, sourness, pungency, bitterness and astringency.

The characteristics of any batch of *sake* is determined by the rice itself, how much of the rice has been milled away, whether or not distilled alcohol is added, the mineral content of the water used in the fermenting process, the amount of yeast, when the yeast is added, how long the process is continued, and, according to experts, some elements that master brewers keep to themselves.

There are four main types of sake, each of which is determined as much by the milling of the rice used as well as the brewing process. These four sake types are:

Junmai-shu (At least 30% of the rice polished away and no distilled alcohol added. This type is referred to as pure rice wine). *Honjozo-shu* (At least 30% of the rice milled away, and some distilled alcohol added).

Ginjo-shu (At least 40% of the rice polished away. When some alcohol is added it is called *Ginjo*. If no alcohol is added it is called *Junmai Ginjo*.)

Daiginjo-shu (At least 50% of rice polished away; again with or without added alcohol; if labeled *Daiginjo*, it means distilled alcohol was added; if labeled *Junmai Daiginjo*, it means no alcohol added).

A fifth type of sake refers to all of the above when they have not been pasteurized, in which case they are called *Namazake*, literally "raw sake."

The first four categories are known as *Tokutei Meishoshu,* or Special Designation Sake. Each category has its own flavor profile based on the brewing methods employed and how much of the rice has been polished away. Sake gourmets pride themselves on being able to distinguish the types by their taste, rather than reading the labels.

Several districts in Japan have been known for the quality of their *sake* since ancient times. These include Nada in Hyogo Prefecture, (now within the city of Kobe), Kyoto and districts in Akita, Nagano and Hiroshima prefectures.

Top sake brands include *Hakutsuru* (Hah-kuu-t'sue-rue) or White Crane, *Ozeki* (Oh-zay-kee), which refers to a sumo champion, and *Gekkeikan* (Gake-kay-e-kahn). Okura Shuzo, the company that produces *Gekkeikan*, was founded in 1637.

Altogether, there are some 3,000 *sake* makers in Japan, most of them producing what is called *jizake* (jee-zah-kay), or local brands.

In addition to "regular" *sake*, there are also sweet, carbonated, dry, hard, and aged varieties. *Sake* is generally heated before drinking to bring out the taste and give it more of an immediate kick. One special type of *sake* is brewed for drinking cold, or on ice.

Sake was traditionally served and drank before meals, not during or after meals. But many people now drink *sake* during their meals and as well as in between meals.

Enormous amounts of *sake* are consumed at gatherings held to enjoy the beauties of nature, especially when viewing cherry blossoms, the full moon, and newly fallen snow.

Like wine experts, s*ake* gourmets claim that they can also identify the region a particular sample of *sake* came from by its taste and aroma.

Visitors to Japan, especially those into sushi who dine at a sushi restaurant, should at least sip a little hot *sake* with their raw fish—it adds enormously to the experience.

[16]
ENKAI !
How to Party Japanese Style!

Until the turn of the 21st century the Japanese had a reputation of being workaholics, of not given to letting their hair down and having a good time. The Japanese were indeed hard workers, but the impression that they didn't go in for parties and other forms of entertainment was way off the mark.

One of the earliest anecdotes in Japan's creation myth is about a party held by one of the gods that became so boisterous he was kicked out of the pantheon as punishment.

He didn't give up partying, however, and apparently passed on his predilections for a good time to the human progeny of the gods. In any event, entertainment of various kinds has been a significant part of Japanese culture since ancient times.

As in virtually all societies, singing, dancing and drinking were major entertainment activities in early Japan, with copious references to them in historical records. Rather than decrease with the passing of time, entertainment of has grown in volume and variety to the point that since the mid-1950s it has been one of Japan's largest industries—if not the largest.

One of the most characteristically Japanese forms of entertainment today is subsumed in the word *enkai* (inn-kigh), which is usually translated as "Japanese style banquet" and is a kind of generic term that refers to a gathering where food and drinks are served, and which serves several purposes.

The first *enkai* of record occurred in the 7th century at the Imperial Court on New Year's Day and on other auspicious occasions during the year. In 1873 the celebration was renamed *Shinnen Enkai* (sheen-nane inn-kigh), or New Year's Banquet, and was held on January 5th.

This was discontinued as an imperial court event after World War II, and was later picked up by the general public as a way of celebrating special occasions any time of the year, including New Years and at the end of the year, when it was called *Bōnen Kai* (bohh-nane kigh), or "Party to Forget the Year" just ending.

Shinnen Kai and *Bōnen Kai* are still held annually by the thousands throughout Japan, but there are dozens of thousands more that are held to celebrate promotions, company events, farewell parties, assignments abroad, political rallies, family gatherings, welcoming parties (for new company or club members), etc.

In earlier times the locations for *enkai* were almost always restaurants or halls that had Japanese style rooms with reed-mat (*tatami*) floors, but now many, especially large ones, are also held in hotel banquet halls that are Western style, with tables and chairs.

The importance of the *enkai* to Japanese can hardly be overstated. They are one of the primary ways the Japanese bond with each other in both formal and informal ways during the proceedings, which generally include a number of short speeches, a great deal of toasting and hand-clapping, and often singing and dancing performances by individuals or groups.

For the Japanese the *enkai* are an institutionalized and ritualized way for them to express and nurture their Japaneseness, to shore up their psyche and energy, and strengthen their bonds with each other and their guests.

Foreign business people can get a lot of cultural mileage out of sponsoring *enkai* for their Japanese affiliations, as well as by attending (when invited) those staged by the Japanese side.

Dinners (and sometimes lunches) arranged for large tourist groups in resort hotels and inns are typically done *enkai* style, with the participants wearing yukata robes, sitting on *tatami* floors at low tables, and being called upon to participate in some kind of entertainment.

Visitors in Japan, for business or pleasure, should make an effort to attend at least one *enkai*. They are a marvelous way to physically, emotionally and spiritually experience the traditional culture.

[17]
Visitors Can Enjoy Japan's Most Popular Pastime

THE FAVORITE pastime in Japan is not shopping, attending sports events, watching television, sightseeing, soaking in hot spring spa baths, or even patronizing the country's huge network of "love hotels."

It is dining out!

There are over 800,000 general eating and drinking establishments in Japan, and if this doesn't seem like a very large number, one has only to recall that the whole country is only about the size of the American state of Montana, and that some 80 percent of this landmass is uninhabited because it is made up of great mountain chains.

This becomes even more significant when it is realized that over 90 percent of Japan's 126 million people live in a combined area about the size of a single county in Montana, Arizona and other western American states.

In Tokyo, Kyoto, Osaka and other major cities there are numerous three-and-four-block districts that have as many as five hundred restaurants of one kind or another. Single buildings often have from ten to thirty or forty restaurants in their basements and on upper floors.

In addition to these fixed restaurants, at any one time throughout the year there are an additional several hundred thousand portable food stalls on the streets selling such things as baked sweet potatoes, *O'den* (a kind of stew), *yakitori* (barbecued chicken on sticks), and *okonomi* (a kind of seafood pancake quiche).

Then there are several thousand *konbini*, or convenience markets, that sell ready-made breakfast, lunch and dinner meals, attracting hundreds of thousands of customers daily.

And if you have the idea that it might be difficult for foreign visitors to find familiar restaurants in Japan, there are some 30,000 American and European restaurants, 61,000 Chinese restaurants and 3,200-plus eating places categorized as Oriental restaurants—not to mention some 4,300 hamburger joints.

Now there is something new that has added a more expansive dimension to dining out in Japan—large food theme parks that seem to be proliferating like, well, like bugs bunny.

While Japan's conventional theme parks have had some tough years since the early 1990s, not so the new breed of food parks. These new dining courts appeal to people across the board, from nearby office workers and shoppers to families that want to eat out in a fun atmosphere at bargain prices.

Food courts [as opposed to food parks] are old hat in Japan. Almost every major office building in the country has its own food court—as do department stores. But this new phenomenon has broadened the food court theme to the park and village concept.

Interestingly, all of the restaurants in some of the food villages serve only dish—like soba noodles or *okonomi*.

The best known and most popular of the *okonomi* theme restaurants is *Okonomi Mura*, or Okonomi Village, in Hiroshima. The "village" takes up three floors in a high-rise building, and attracts over one million diners a year, including thousands of foreign visitors. As of this writing, the other top nine food theme "villages" and "parks" in the country are:

Ramen Stadium, in Fukuoka (ramen noodles)

Shin-Yokohama Ramen Museum, in Yokohama (ramen noodles)

Yokohama Curry Museum, in Yokohama (curry dishes)

Naniwa Kuishinbo Yokocho, in Osaka (variety of Osaka specialties)

Shimizu Sushi Museum, in Shizuoka (sushi from nearby port of Shimizu)

Ramen Yokocho Shichifukujin, in Hiroshima (ramen in Showa era shops)

Ramen Jokamachi, in Kumamoto ("castle city" style ramen)

Ikebukuro Gyoza Stadium, in Tokyo (different styles of deep-fried dumplings)

Jiyugaoka Sweets Forest, in Tokyo (confections to die for)

Foreign visitors cannot say that they have really "done Japan" if they have not sampled one of the new food villages. The insights they offer into elements of traditional Japanese culture are a major part of the value of visiting Japan.

For a definitive guide to restaurants and dining in Japan see my book, *DINING GUIDE TO JAPAN – Find the Right Restaurant, Order the Right Dish, and Pay the Right Price!*

[18]
"Vistas Fit For The Eyes of Kings"

NOT MANY people go to Japan to enjoy the scenic beauty of the islands. They are much more likely to think in terms of such images as the country's famous cherry blossoms, geisha, kabuki, the snow-capped peak of Mt. Fuji, huge loin-clothed sumo wrestlers, or even the opportunity to do some shopping for high-tech products in Akihabara, Tokyo's famed "Electric Town."

But they will miss out on an opportunity of a lifetime if they do not make a point of experiencing some of the natural beauty that Japan offers.

Of course, most countries are blessed with areas of extraordinary scenic beauty—some so sublime that they inspire the poetic muse and induce spiritual ecstasy. But few countries in the world surpass Japan in the sheer volume and variety of its natural beauty.

The islands of Japan owe their extraordinary scenic beauty to their volcanic peaks and central mountains chains that have smaller chains radiating out toward the coasts, resulting in numerous narrow valleys and small coastal plains separated from each other by ridges and headlands.

The greatest of these natural mountain ranges are on the main island of Honshu, and are characterized by peaks up to 3,000 meters (9,000 feet) and more in height. While these and other mountains are grand in size and form, it is the volcanic mountains that provide the special flavor of the country's topography.

Altogether, there are seven great volcanic systems, with some 200 volcanoes, running through the islands—and

Japan has one-tenth of the world's active volcanoes. Of course, Fuji san (Mt. Fuji) is the mother of all volcanoes in Japan, and although it last erupted in 1707, it is still alive, and recently has been grumbling and quivering.

One hundred kilometers (62 miles) southwest of Tokyo, Mt. Fuji is so high (3,776 meters / 12,385 ft.) that it is visible within a radius of some 200 miles. The base of Mt. Fuji is so massive that extends into several prefectures. Part way up the great cone there are a chain of five lakes that encircle the mountain, adding to its scenic ambiance and its attraction as a recreational destination.

Because Mt. Fuji towers over central Honshu like a great sentinel, it gets most of the praise, but it is in the coastlines of Japan that nature outdid itself. The islands have a total of 16,120 miles of seacoast that alternates between white sand beaches generally bordered by groves of gnarled pine trees, precipitous cliffs also clad in pines, lagoon-like bays dotted with emerald islets, secluded coves and inlets bounded by jagged walls of stone, caves, natural "bridges" of stone, and sculptured rock formations that are literally beyond the hand of man.

The central chains of mountains that make up the bulk of Japan give rise to thousands of streams and dozens of large rivers that course down gorges and ravines that are so beautiful the more finely attuned viewer may become intoxicated. The islands are also rich in lakes.

Outside of its cities, Japan is heavily forested. In the spring and summer the country is covered in a great blanket of green. In the fall, the leaves of great swatches of deciduous trees turn brown, gold and red. In winter, the high country and northern regions are sheathed in deep layers of snow that turn them into white wonderlands.

The natural beauty of Japan has long been celebrated in poetry, song and the arts, and has played an integral role in the life of the people, not only in their aesthetic practices but also in the their religious and philosophical life. The founders of the thousands of Buddhist temples and Shinto shrines in the country deliberately sought out places of exceptional beauty for their location.

Long ago someone described the *Seto Naikai* (Inland Sea), the shallow body of ocean that separates the islands of Honshu, Shikoku and Kyushu, as "A sight fit for the eyes of kings!" And it is just one of many such sights throughout Japan.

Visitors and residents alike who do not avail themselves of the opportunity to gaze upon some of the earth's grandest scenery are missing one of the great pleasures of life.

[19]
Japan's Hot Spring Spas Add Erotic Spice to Life

SEVERAL HUNDRED million years ago the earth's mantle opened up and spewed forth the landmass that makes up the Japanese islands, leaving a ring of volcanoes and thermal vents from the northernmost island of Hokkaido to the southern island of Kyushu.

Present-day Japan has 10 percent of the earth's volcanoes and more active volcanoes than any other country. There are more than 10,000 well-known thermal vents in the crust of Japan, and over 2,100 of these have been developed into *onsen* (own-sen), or hot spring bath spas.

Japan's hot spring spas can be found in mountain gorges and valleys, on the waists of mountains, along the sides of peninsulas, and on the coasts. Some hot springs bubble up from the seabed offshore. There is one in the middle of Tokyo Bay that has been tapped for a new, spectacular hot spring spa complex on the man-made island of Odaiba.

The larger of the hot springs vents have given birth to hundreds of resort villages and towns. Some of them, like Atami, Beppu and Ito, qualify as cities.

Smaller *onsen* have 15 to 30 inns and hotels that feature hot mineral baths and the other amenities of a Japanese style spa. Larger *onsen* have from 30 to 300 inns and hotels. The largest one, Beppu, has some 700 inns and attracts upwards of a million visitors a year.

Hokkaido alone has 193 onsen spas, and over 1,500 thermal springs. Shizuoka Prefecture, about an hour south of Tokyo by Bullet Train, has only 71 hot spring resort spas, but together they have over 2,100 thermal springs.

Hundreds of Japan's thermal springs have been in commercial use as spas for at least 1,500 years. Numerous events of special significance that occurred in the baths have made the history books. One of the more interesting: Yoritomo Minamoto, the founder in 1192 of Japan's shogunate form of government was a regular visitor. His favorite: Kusatsu [Kuu-sot-t'sue], in Gunma Prefecture northwest of present-day Tokyo, because the high mineral content of its waters made his rheumatism better.

During the famous Tokugawa Shogunate era (1603-1867), successive Shoguns had water brought from the Kusatsu springs to Edo (Tokyo) for their daily baths.

All of the 2,000-plus hot spring spas that are members of the *Japan Spa Association* have had their waters analyzed for their mineral content, and provide specific details on their efficacy in curing and relieving a variety of physical and mental illnesses.

In the last century, Japan's *onsen* have gone from being just health resorts catering to those with problems to being both health and recreational destinations, with a variety of activities and facilities.

Today, *onsen* spas attract huge numbers of regular vacationers, including families, as well as honeymooners and lovers. Many people go to *onsen* for days or weeks when they are doing some kind of work project that requires peace and quiet. Others use them as retreats, when they want to opt out of the hubbub of urban life for a weekend or longer.

For the last century, the spas around Lake Hakone, an hour's train ride from Tokyo and adjoining Mt. Fuji, have attracted many foreign notables. There is almost always a sprinkling of foreign visitors at all major hot spring spas, particularly those in the vicinity of Tokyo, Nagoya, Kyoto, Osaka and Kobe.

Some *onsen* feature *rotenburo* (roh-tane-buu-roh) or outside baths that look like small, shallow swimming pools set among picturesque volcanic boulders. Many of the *rotenburo* have magnificent views of the surrounding areas.

Mixed-sex bathing is still practiced in some hot spring spas, but not in local public *onsen*. All resort spas have private baths for couples and families. [Regular TV promotional travel stories on the country's spas often show men and women bathing together in large communal baths—with their modesty protected by small *tenugui* (tay-nuu-gooey) hand towels covering key body parts.]

For many foreign tourists a visit to a hot spring spa is the highlight of their trip. The foreign visitor who leaves Japan without having had the hot spring spa experience has missed a major opportunity to enjoy one of the special pleasures the country has to offer.

For the visitor who cannot get beyond Tokyo, there is *Oedo Onsen Monogatari* (Oh-eh-doh Own-sen Moe-no-gah-tah-ree) on Odaiba islet in Tokyo Bay, only a few minutes from Shimbashi Station in the center of the city.

This huge complex is built as an Edo era *onsen* village, with restaurants and shops that are right out of the Tokugawa Shogunate period of Japan.

Trains going to Odaiba leave Shimbashi Station every few minutes via the famous Rainbow Bridge that connects the mainland with the small islet in the bay. The train trip to the island takes only about eight minutes.

Even if you don't indulge in the special pleasure of a hot spring bath on the island its other attractions, from shopping to food courts, make the trip an extraordinary experience.

[20]
Vacationers, Honeymooners, Lovers, Fugitives Flock to Hot Springs

HOT SPRINGS have played a vital role in the history of Japan, not only for their contribution to the Japanese obsession with cleanliness and their medicinal benefits, but also as popular venues for planning political intrigues and strategies, for vacationers seeking release from the stresses of daily life, for honeymooners and lovers seeking the anonymity of their secluded locations and the lustration effects of hot baths...even miscreants who have committed some crime and find solace in soaking in hot mineral water.

Japanese novelists and filmmakers have long used the special attraction of hot springs as locales for their stories.

Hot springs are, in fact, one of Japan's most important cultural and economic assets, on a par with the country's arts and crafts, industrial technology and many manufacturing industries.

Some years ago the U.S. Geological Survey did a worldwide survey of hot springs and mineral springs and found that Japan led the world in the number of *onsen*. According to the U.S.G.S report, France has 124 hot springs, Italy 149, the United States 1,003, and Japan 2,237.

Fudoki (fuu-doh-kee), the ancient regional chronicles of Japan, note that prehistoric emperors were devotees of hot spring bathing, and that Buddhist priests traveled to the far reaches of the country promoting the efficacy of hot spring bathing and encouraging their commercial development because bathing daily was an integral part of Buddhist purification rituals.

Japan's creation myths attribute the number of hot springs in Japan to two gods of medicine (*Okuninushi* and *Sukunahikona*) who caused the springs to gush forth from the bowels of the Earth for the benefit of the people...and these two divine beings are enshrined at many *onsen* around the country.

Dogo Hot Springs, in what is now Ehime Prefecture on Shikoku Island, is believed to have been the first *onsen* developed as a spa in Japan, and is said to be where some legendary emperors, (prior to 300 A.D.) did their bathing.

In earlier times in addition to their daily baths at home and in public bathhouses all classes of Japanese engaged in special ritualistic bathing at hot springs several times a year. These events included a New Year's Bath, Mid-Winter Bath, Spring Bath Cure, Bon Festival Bath, Pre-Harvest Bath, Post-Harvest Bath, Autumn Bath Cure and Winter Bath Cure.

Interestingly, the water at all of Japan's hot springs is not naturally hot. According to Japanese law, a hot spring must have a specified amount of minerals and other ingredients to be designated a hot spring, but mineralized water that comes out of the ground at 25 degrees centigrade (77 degrees F.) warrants being defined as a hot spring.

One of the hottest hot springs in Japan is *Kusatsu Onsen*, where the water is a steady 48 degrees C. (118 degrees F.), which is so hot that bathers are limited to three minutes at a time. The *onsen* attracts visitors from all over Japan who go there for the therapeutic benefits resulting from repeated immersions in the water. A regular "course" consists of four 3-minute immersions per day.

Kusatsu Onsen is in Gumma Prefecture about 90 minutes north of Tokyo. It has been in use since the 1100s.

Foreign visitors who would like to experience the ambience and benefits of Japan's *onsen* might want to keep in mind that there are several different types of baths at different resort spas.

Among them: *hohmatsuyoku* (hoh-maht-sue-yoe-kuu), a bath that is filled with air bubbles to massage the body; *utaseyu* (uu-tah-say-yuu), in which the water falls from a height onto the bather's body (like standing under a waterfall); *rotenburo* (roh-tane-buu-roh), which are outside open air baths, *mushiburo* (muu-she-buu-roh), like a sauna; *zabonburo* (zah-bone-buu-roh), which is a bath in which a special kind of oranges have been squished; and *sunamushiyu* (suu-nah-muu-she-yuu) or a hot, wet sand bath.

And as previously mentioned, many of Japan's most popular hot spring spas are popular because they feature mixed-sex bathing. That beats basting in hot sand any day.

[21]
The Story Behind Japan's Famous "Bullet Trains"

ON OCTOBER 1, 1964 Japan National Railways (JNR) inaugurated the world's fastest trains, which were quickly dubbed Bullet Trains by the foreign news media because of their shape and speed. Their success revolutionized thinking about modern railroads.

The new high-speed train service, between Tokyo and Osaka, began as a concept in 1956 when a committee was established to study the challenge of improving train service, already operating well beyond its rated capacity, between these two important cities.

The first recommendation of the committee in 1957 was that the existing double-track line should be expanded to a four-track line. The following year, a second committee voted to add a high-speed railroad on a separate double-track.

Ground was broken on this historic undertaking in April 1959, with a proposed completion date of mid-1964, in time for the fall opening of the Tokyo Olympics. Approximately 30 kilometers (18.6 miles) of the line was completed in 1962 for test purposes. Two sets of prototype trains were tested on the track over the next two years to prove the technology and identify the optimum design features.

The construction of the entire line was completed in July 1964. When full service was begun on October 1, it cut the travel time between Tokyo and Osaka from 6 hours and 30 minutes to 3 hours and 10 minutes—a factor that dramatically influenced business trips between the two cities.

The new Bullet Trains, which had a maximum speed of 210 kilometers (130 mph) and cruised at 127 mph, were an instant hit with both the Japanese public and foreign visitors. Daily service began with 60 trains, each with 12 coaches. Many Japanese and foreign residents booked passage on the trains just for the experience. Within the first 13 months, service on the new line was increased to 110 trains daily to handle the crowds.

The 1964 fall Olympics in Tokyo resulted in massive international news coverage for the new line, known in Japanese as *Shinkansen* (Sheen-kahn-sen), which translates as a very mundane "New Trunk Line."

The Bullet Train track was a conventional ballasted track, elevated on embankments or viaducts for the entire route, using 60 kilograms per meter (121 lbs per yard) welded rail, on pre-stressed concrete ties.

The coaches were multi-unit electric cars, selected over locomotive-hauled cars in order to achieve more even distribution of axle load and less stress on the track structure; to make it possible to apply dynamic brakes to all axles via the motors, to simplify the turn-around process, and to prevent the failure of one or two units interrupting the entire train.

Each single wheel axle had its own DC motor; each coach had two trucks with two axles each, for a total of four motors per car, and 64 for each train—making it possible to apply brakes on all axles at the same time.

The whole system was electrified with 25,000 volts at 60 hertz. But oddly enough, the commercial power frequency in Tokyo and for 150 km (93 mi) west of the city is 50 hertz, making it necessary to install frequency converters at two locations on the trains.

Electric power substations were erected every 50 kilometers (32 mi) along the high-speed route, with a special phase break system that switched power automatically from one station to the next so that trains could go through the switchovers with their propulsion power on.

The new Bullet Trains were operated with a system called Automatic Train Control (ATC) to prevent collisions by maintaining a safe distance between trains. The permissible speed was automatically indicated in the cab according to the distance between trains, the proximity of the next station stop, and the condition of the track.

These speed limits were set at 0, 30, 70, 110, 160, and 210 kilometers. The speed was left to the discretion of the conductor, but the brakes went on automatically if the train exceeded the permissible limits. The operator also brought the trains to a stop at the stations after receiving the 30 km per hour signal.

Following the inauguration of Bullet Train service between Tokyo and Osaka, the same high-speed service was expanded to cover the country in a network that became the envy of the world – and for the first several decades of their operation, there was not a single fatal accident anywhere on the network.

By 2007 the fastest Bullet Trains were cruising at 300 kilometers per hour (186.4 mph), and made the Tokyo-Osaka trip in two hours and thirty minutes. As in the past, you can practically set your watch by the departure and arrival of the famous Bulletin Trains. Even a delay of less than a minute calls for an apology to passengers.

The latest generations of trains are electro-magnetically elevated, and cruise at some 300 miles per hour.

Altogether, Japan's bus, subway and train transportation systems are among the best in the world. Some say they are *the* best. They are all user friendly, with an eye for the convenience of foreign visitors who do not read or speak Japanese.

[22]
Japan's Amazing Abundance of Annual Festivals

DESPITE JAPAN'S infrastructure of modernity, from its city skylines and "Bullet Trains" to its millions of people who seem to have high-tech cell phones glued to their ears, traditional Japan still exists in a huge network of inns and restaurants, and in arts, crafts and customs that have not changed in over a thousand years.

One of the most extraordinary historical legacies that has been kept alive in Japan is its *matsuri* (mot-sue-ree) or festivals. I don't know if anyone has ever actually counted them, but every village, town and city in the country, as well as thousands of temples and shrines throughout the country, have one or more annual festivals.

A very limited calendar of festivals that are considered of special interest to foreign visitors (published by the Japan Travel Bureau) lists a total of 271 annual festivals. Travel books in English generally list only the Big 8, or the Big 10 or some such small number that take place in the largest cities and are regarded more or less as national events.

There are, in fact, 13 festivals in Japan that are national holidays, some of which last for several days. *Shogatsu* (Show-got-sue) or New Years, which is regarded as a festival, officially beings on the eve of December 31, and ends on January 7th, although large numbers of people take additional days off.

The reason for the large number and variety of *matsuri* in Japan can be traced to tenets of Shintoism, the indigenous religion, which holds that all things in nature—trees, rocks, mountains, water, whatever—have spirits, and that people must remain on good terms with all these spirits to prevent evil and destructive things from happening.

Since the economy of Japan was agricultural until the last decades of the 19th century, the livelihood of the people was greatly influenced by rain, wind and the seasons, leading to year-around religious rituals designed to placate and please the spirits of nature.

Matsuri to help ward off diseases and other calamities also became common. Some festivals had to do with ensuring fertility; others were designed to bring peace to the spirits of physical things—one such thing being broken and discarded needles.

The purpose of the festivals was to invite the appropriate deities to come down from Heaven so the people could pray to them directly, and in keeping with their cultural programming to structure everything, the Japanese designed their *matsuri* to have three parts.

The first part of a festival is called *kami mukae* (kah-me muu-kigh), or "meeting the gods," which is a ceremony held at a shrine or other sacred place to welcome the gods to the Earth. The deity concerned descends from Heaven and takes up temporary residence in a palanquin-like portable shrine called a *mikoshi* (me-koh-she).

The second part of a festival, called *shinkoh* (sheen-koh), consists of participants carrying the *mikoshi* around rural communities and through the streets of towns and cities, generally with chants and some kind of music.

The third part of a *matsuri* is the *kami okuri* (kah-me oh-kuu-ree), or "god send-off," a ritual to send the gods back to Heaven.

Other *matsuri* are designed to commemorate major events in history, and are the equivalent of the float parades so popular in the U.S., with people dressed in period costumes marching in long columns, along with carts and palanquins from the era concerned.

Among the most popular of Japan's annual festivals are the *odori matsuri* (oh-doh-ree mot-sue-ree) or dance festivals, in which participants wearing colorful yukata robes and traditional sedge hats dance through the streets.

Paper lanterns, huge drums, gongs, masks, dolls and other historical images are a big part of many Japanese festivals, as are fireworks.

Kyoto is especially famous for its festivals, some of which date back to the 8th and 9th centuries and go on for days. Its *Gion Matsuri*, for example, staged by the Yasaka Shrine, begins on July 1 and lasts until July 29th. *Gion* (ghee-own) is a district in Kyoto that is famous for its geisha houses. The biggest *Gion* events occur on July 16 and 17.

Kyoto's biggest fall festival is the *Jidai Matsuri* (Jee-die Mot-sue-re), which means Festival of the Ages. It occurs in the latter part of October, and depicts Japan from the 19th century back to the 8th century, with some 1,700 marchers divided into 20 groups.

Japan has a number of curious festivals that attract large audiences. Among them: mud-slinging, paying homage to phallic images, eating and drinking from huge bowls, listening to the voices of dead relatives, watching the training of priests, viewing parades by jokers and clown, and *matsuri* in which the participants laugh and laugh and laugh, until they are rid of all stress and ill-feelings. It beats going to a shrink!

There are a number of festivals that feature huge replicas of the male organ, carved from wood logs and appropriately painted that attract large crowds of people of all ages and genders. The real-looking penises are carried through the streets on carts or wagons pulled by teams of men.

Vendors offer small purse-size replicas of penises to women who want to become pregnant to buy and take home with them.

[23]
Celebrating New Year's the Japanese Way

AMONG JAPAN'S dozens of annual celebrations and hundreds of festivals, *Omisoka* (Oh-me-soh-kah) and *Shogatsu* (Show-got-sue) stand out as the most significant hallmarks of the passage of time and the importance of cultural observations.

Omisoka means New Year's Eve or the last day of the year. *Shogatsu* means New Year, New Year's Day, and January 1st all rolled into one.

Shogatsu, which is the first day of several days of special events, is the most important celebration period in Japan—with the celebrations beginning on New Year's Eve.

The two major New Year's Eve events are *Joya no Kane* (Joh-yah no Kah-nay) and *Hatsumode* (Hot-sue-moh-day).

Joya by itself is another term for New Year's Eve, and the *kane* in *Joya no Kane* refers to temple bells. *Joya no kane* may therefore be translated as "Ringing in the New Year."

On New Year's Eve crowds make their way to temples that have huge bells. As midnight approaches, gangs of young men dressed in traditional loincloths (despite the frigid temperatures in the central and northern portions of the islands) take turns swinging large suspended log clappers against the temple bells a total of 108 times—108 being the number of sins said by Buddhism to afflict mankind.

The idea is that each time a temple bell is rung one of the built-in sins is eliminated. Great effort is made to time the last of the 108 rings with the stroke of midnight and the end of the old year so that everyone begins the new year with a clean slate—a ritual that has been followed for centuries.

At a number of more famous shrines and temples around the country, this annual ritual is shown on television locally and nationwide, and is viewed by millions in their homes and in public places. At the stroke of midnight, those in pubs and other such places mark the end of *Omisoka* and the beginning of *Shogatsu* with shouts and toasts.

Hatsumode, the second major New Year's ritual, can be translated as "First Visit," and refers specifically to the age-old custom of going to a shrine or temple between midnight on New Year's Eve and January 7 to pray for health and happiness during the new year.

Huge numbers of people begin heading toward shrines or temples sometime before midnight, with the idea of reaching the shrine or temple just before or precisely at 12 a.m.

In Tokyo the favored destination of hundreds of thousands of people is the famous Meiji Shrine in a wooded park on the west side of Harajuku Station on the city's Yamanote Loop Line. Thousands of people arrive in Harajuku on the Yamanote train line. Others arrive via the Chiyoda Subway Line's adjoining Meiji Jingumae subway station.

But dozens of thousands of subway commuters prefer to disembark at Omotesando Station (the station just before Meiji Jingu Mae) and walk down the wide Omotesando Boulevard to the entrance to the shrine grounds.

 This is the approach that I recommend—which should be done in the company of one or more good friends—because it adds a special dimension to the experience. One thing to keep in mind, however, is that as midnight approaches on New Year's Eve in Tokyo it can be cold enough to freeze the *kintama* off of a brass monkey; so really warm clothing is advised.

Other New Year's customs: sending out gifts to people important to you; cleaning house before the end of the year; paying off all debts; sending New Year greeting cards to family members, friends and co-workers; eating *omochi* (oh-moe-chee) rice cakes; eating buckwheat noodles on New Year's Eve (because they are believed to help ensure a long life); and going out to nightclubs, pubs and other places of entertainment to whoop it up with friends.

Travelers in Japan over New Year's should make a point of visiting a shrine or temple on January 1 or on one of the first few days of the New Year. Young children and young women visiting shrines and temples on this day typically dress in their most colorful kimono, there are street stalls galore, and the whole of Japan has a festive look and feel.

Among the most popular of these places in Tokyo: the huge Sensoji Temple complex in Asakusa Ward, the northeastern end of the Ginza Subway Line, about 20 subway minutes from central Tokyo. The long mall leading to the shrine is flanked by a hundred or more retail stalls.

All of Tokyo's popular night-time entertainment districts—Akasaka, Aoyama, the Ginza, Ikebukuro, Roppongi, Shibuya, Shinjuku, etc.—are packed on New Year's Eve.

[24]
The Wonder That Was (and is) Tokyo!

JAPAN HAS MORE cities with populations of 500,000 and above than any other country in the world except for the United States. This remarkable fact was (or is) a direct result of the early proliferation of shrines and temples in Japan, and the construction of a large number of castles by provincial fief lords in the 16th and 17th centuries.

From the beginning of urban life in Japan virtually every township, village and community had its Shinto shrine. Many of these shrines, such as the one at Ise, were large, elaborate complexes that attracted worshippers from afar.

Following the introduction of Buddhism into Japan in the 6th century A.D., Buddhist monks traveled to the far reaches of the islands, building temples in places that were especially scenic—from seacoasts to mountain sites. Many of these Buddhist temples were larger and more elaborate than the numerous Shinto shrines.

Throughout Japan's early history territorial warlords and fief rulers built and maintained military forts and castle-like structures, but true castles did not appear until latter part of the 1500s, which was marked by an amazing flurry of castle-building on a scale never before seen in any country.

The larger and more famous of these shrines, temples and castles required large numbers of people to maintain them and to provide services to visitors, resulting in the formation of villages that became towns and towns that became cities. The most extraordinary example of this village-to-city phenomenon was that of Edo (present-day Tokyo).

Edo, which is variously translated as "River Gate" or "Bay Door," entered Japanese history in the 12th century when a regional chieftain named Shigenaga Edo built a fort in the vicinity of a village that had long existed on the edge of Hibiya Cove, where the inhabitants used *hibi* (hee-bee) or bamboo structures, to farm edible sea plants.

At that time, the area consisted of marshes, valleys and rivers that emptied into the bay, and was divided by five low hills that later came to be known as Shinagawa, Azabu, Kojimachi, Hongo and Ueno [all famous districts in present-day Tokyo.]

In 1457 a man named Dokan Ota, a retainer of the regional warlord, built an elaborate (for the times) castle on the site of the original Edo fort, which set on a prominence overlooking Hibiya Cove. It quickly became the most famous castle in the Kanto region at that time, only to be abandoned in 1486 when Ota's own overlord had him assassinated.

In 1590 the soon to be great Ieyasu Tokugawa established his military headquarters on the site of the old Edo Castle. In addition to continuing his battle to become the supreme military leader in Japan, Ieyasu had a new, larger and more elaborate castle constructed on the site. He also ordered his staff to begin working on a layout for the new city he envisioned.

Successful in his battles against competing warlords in 1603, Ieyasu moved quickly to make Edo the administrative capital of Japan, with Edo Castle as the headquarters of the new Tokugawa Shogunate.

The population of Edo grew with astounding speed. Ieyasu's huge army of warriors was quickly joined by their families, along with dozens of thousands of trades people and carpenters who set about building a city.

But the building was not helter-skelter. The master plan for the new Shogunate capital was a spiral. An area adjoining the castle on the east and northeast was reserved exclusively for the residences and retainers of provincial lords who had supported Ieyasu in his early battles.

A large swath adjoining the castle grounds on the south and southwest was reserved for fief lords who had opposed him or had become his allies only in the last major battle.

The area adjoining the castle grounds on the west and north was allocated to Ieyasu's retainers and samurai warriors. The east and southeast portions of the spiral-shaped divisions were assigned to ordinary townspeople.

Within the area designated for ordinary people there were further subdivisions, with carpenters, stonemasons, furniture makers and other specialty groups living in their own areas. Not one to scant on security, Ieyasu had pockets of his own warriors placed strategically throughout the city.

Five great roads, radiating out like spokes from the inner moat surrounding Edo Castle, were constructed to accommodate traffic within and to the city. The building of the new city required dozens of thousands of workmen to cut and deliver trees and stones to the construction sites.

Hills were leveled or dramatically reduced in size and height to provide building sites and landfill to reclaim the swamp areas. It was a glorious time to be in Edo.

Ieyasu's grandson, Iemitsu, who became Shogun in 1623, took another extraordinary step in 1635 that was to be the centerpiece of the Shogunate and life in Japan for the next 227 years. He mandated that some 260 of the country's fief lords would move their wives and children to Edo, and themselves spend every other year there in attendance at the Shogun's Court.

Each lord was required to build and maintain three mansions in Edo, and to keep them fully staffed the year around. This resulted in another great influx of people into the city. It also resulted in the lords competing with each other in the size and grandeur of their mansions and landscaped gardens. The grounds and gardens of the richer lords were immense.

By 1700, Edo had a population of 1.5 million, making it by far the largest city on earth (London, the next largest city, had only 800,000 residents). And for the next 160 years Edo was surely the world's best ordered, cleanest, most colorful, and most sophisticated city.

Modern-day Tokyo has become a huge hodgepodge of villages and towns that grew together, but it still ranks as one of the world's greatest cities, and few, if any, can match it in the quantity and diversity of its arts, crafts, entertainment, food, and vitality.

Dozens of Tokyo's largest districts, included Asakusa, Ginza, Harajuku, Ikebukuro, Kanda, Roppongi, Shibuya and Shinjuku, are cities within themselves, each with its own distinct character and personality.

The names of hundreds of districts and areas in the city are linked with the fief lords who built their mansions there and the variety of craftsmen and shopkeepers who flocked around them, making every neighborhood a living lesson in history.

The New Otani boasts an amazing landscaped garden created by a fief lord during the Tokugawa Shogunate era. The Sheraton Miyako is next door to one of the largest of these amazing sights.

[25]
View from the Top of Tokyo

EVERY YEAR some quarter of a million people climb to the top of Japan's famed Mt. Fuji to get a fantastic view of a big chunk of the country, including Tokyo in the distance.

There are much easier and faster ways to get a bird's eye view of Tokyo that are only a few minutes from any part of the city, and can be reached by elevator. First is the landmark Tokyo Tower, which at 333 meters in height (1,093 ft.) is higher than France's Eiffel Tower.

Built in 1958 to facilitate radio and television broadcasting, Tokyo Tower has two observation decks, one 150 meters above ground and the other at the 250-meter level, making it one of the highest observation decks in the world.

Located on one of the many low hills that dot the south and southwestern portions of Tokyo, which adds to its height above sea-level, the tower was an instant hit with city residents and visitors alike because at the time of its construction there were no high-rise structures in the city.

Both of the tower's observation decks are equipped with fixed telescopes for close-up views of the sprawling city, but one of the most popular views from the decks doesn't require a telescope.

On clear days, the towering pinnacle of Mt. Fuji can be seen to the southwest, 100 kilometers (62 mi.) away, adjoining the shores of Suruga Bay. [Visitors flying into Japan have reported sighting the snow-clad peak of Mt. Fuji when they were still 300 miles out.]

But the views from Tokyo Tower that are the most interesting—and useful—are those of the city itself, because they provide viewers with an opportunity to see the layout of the sprawling metropolis, which, from ground level, can be more confusing than a maze.

Among the most prominent of the several dozen major "centers" that make up the city that are identifiable from the observation decks are the Imperial Palace grounds, Nagata-cho (government center), the famous Ginza shopping and entertainment district, "hotel center" in Minato Ward, the wild and wooly Roppongi entertainment district, the Marunouchi, Otemachi and Nihonbashi business districts, the forest of high-rise office buildings in the Shinjuku district, the young people's entertainment and shopping havens of Harajuku and Shibuya, and Ikebukuro with its towering Sunshine Building in the northwestern portion of the city.

And that is not the half of it. You can also see the Akasaka geisha district, the shopping and entertainment mecca of Asakusa which until 1956 boasted one of the world's largest and most elaborate red-light districts, and the imposing sumo stadium in Ryogoku.

Then there is Tokyo Bay with its man-made island of Odaiba that is noted for its shops, restaurants and hot spring spa; along with Disneyland on the northeastern edge of the bay, Haneda Airport, the famous Meiji Jingu Shrine, and more...including Yokohama and other nearby cities.

The ground and lower levels of the Tokyo Tower complex include a variety of gift shops and restaurants, plus a large wax museum that features replicas of famous personages.

The tower complex is within walking distance of several subway stations, including Kamiyacho on the Hibiya Line, Roppongi 1-chome on the Nanboku Line, and Onarimon and Shiba Koen stations on the Toei Mita Line.

It is within 5 to 10 taxi minutes from more than a dozen of the city's leading hotels.

While most visitors to Tokyo Tower automatically go during the day, the night-time views of the city from its observation decks are spectacular and have an ambiance that is totally different from the daytime views…making it one of the top romantic spots in the city for couples.

But this remarkable Tokyo landmark has been eclipsed by a higher high-tech tower that is far grander and far higher than its predecessor. This new landmark is the Tokyo Sky Tree, located in Sumida Ward a short distance from the famous Asakusa entertainment district at the end of the Ginza Subway Line on the northeast side of the city.

At a height of 610 meters [just over 2,000 feet], the Tokyo Sky Tree has a beautifully landscaped three-part plaza-base that spans 400 meters from east to west, connecting Oshiage Station and Narihirabashi Station, and adjoining a river and a park.

There are two observation floors on the Sky Tree—the first one at 350 meters and the second one at 450 meters. Both floors include shopping and restaurant malls.

The highest structure in Japan, and one of the highest in the world, the plan for Tokyo Sky Tree was hatched in 2006 by Japan's top broadcasting companies. Construction began in 2008, with the completion date set for December 2011 and the Grand Opening in the spring of 2012.

If you want to see a photograph of this amazing sight—surely one of the most aesthetically pleasing examples of architectural perfection anywhere in the world—go to Google and type in Tokyo Sky Tree.

Oshiage Station is on the Toei Asakusa Subway Line. Narihirabashi is on the Tobu Isesaki Line. The Sky Tree is about a minute walk from Narihirabashi Station and a short stroll from Oshiage.

[26]
The Wonder That was (and is) Kyoto!

JAPAN'S IMPERIAL capital was moved from Nara to what is now Kyoto in 794 A.D. Within a decade, the new capital had become the wellspring of the arts, crafts and culture that was to distinguish the Japanese for centuries to come…and one of the largest, most sophisticated, and most attractive cities in the world.

The site where the new capital was located was first settled in the 6th century by the Hata family, immigrants from Korea, whose members were skilled in silkworm culture and silk weaving.

Geographically the area consisted of a fault basin, framed on the north, east and west by the Tamba Mountains. Two rivers, now known as the Kamogawa and the Katsuragawa, flowed down from the mountains, bisecting the basin before joining the Yodogawa (Yodo River), which emptied into Osaka Bay.

With the rivers providing easy access to the merchants and markets of Osaka, The Hatas gradually amassed great wealth through commerce in silk goods. Their success attracted the powerful Kamo, Izumo and Ono families who built imposing residences in the northern districts of the basin.

The population of the basin and the wealth of the families living there continued to grow. In the late 700s the reigning emperor and his ministers decided to move the Imperial capital from nearby Nara to the Kyoto basin. They chose to pattern the layout of the new capital after the Tang dynasty Chinese capital of Chang'an (modern Xi'an or Sian), which at that time was one of the largest and grandest cities in the world.

The new capital, christened Heiankyo (literally, Peace Capital), was laid out in the shape of a rectangle, measuring 4.5 kilometers (2.8 miles) from east to west, and 5.2 kilometers (3.2 miles) from north to south. The emperor and his entourage moved to the new city in 794, beginning a golden age in Japan that later came to be known as the *Heian Jidai* (Hay-ee-on Jee-die) or the *Age of Peace*.

Leaders of the powerful Fujiwara and Taira clans, which vied for control of the Imperial Court by providing Imperial consorts and ministers, built their residences in the Shirakawa and Rokuhara districts of central Kyoto.

Other palatial residences and landscaped gardens proliferated. The arts and crafts achieved new heights of sophistication. For the next four centuries, Kyoto flourished as one of the brightest stars in the civilized world.

In 1185 clan leader Yoritomo Minamoto defeated his rivals in battle, had himself named Shogun by the emperor, took complete control of the country, and moved the administrative functions of the government from Kyoto to Kamakura, a tiny seaside village 45 km (28 mi.) southwest of present-day Tokyo. Although no longer the seat of administrative power, Kyoto continued to play a major role in the cultural life of the country.

When the Kamakura government was replaced by the Muromachi Shogunate in 1333, the administration of the country was returned to Kyoto. One of the first things the new government did was to break the hold that Buddhist organizations in Nara had on the building of new temples, and sponsor the building of dozens of temples, many of them huge complexes, within the new city and on the surrounding mountains.

The Muromachi period ended in 1568 after a long civil war that devastated much of the splendid capital. In 1590, Hideyoshi Toyotomi, the winner in this new clan struggle, began a major rebuilding program in Kyoto that included the beautiful Fushimi Castle and the lavishly decorated Jurakudai Mansion.

Ieyasu Tokugawa, Toyotomi's successor, who founded the Tokugawa Shogunate in Edo (now Tokyo) in 1603, continued to support Kyoto as the Imperial as well as the cultural capital of Japan. To accommodate himself on his regular trips to the city, Ieyasu commissioned the building of the famous Nijo Castle, which remains today as one of Kyoto's great treasures.

The arts, crafts and commerce in general flourished in Kyoto during the Tokugawa period, but after the Shogunate fell and the Emperor was restored to power in 1868, the new central government moved the Imperial Court to Tokyo, once again leaving Kyoto on the sidelines of history.

But being shunted aside was to turn out to be a major advantage for Kyoto as the new government in Tokyo led the rest of the country in a rapid industrial revolution between 1870 and 1890. During these two frenetic and sub-sequent decades, Kyoto remained very much like it had been for generations—its castles, palaces, shrines, temples and traditional homes and shops intact.

At the beginning of the U.S.-Japan war in 1941, Kyoto's reputation for its cultural and historical significance was such that American scholars and others who were intimately familiar with the city persuaded the U.S. government to put it off-limits to Allied bombers during the conflict.

Still today, despite its postwar industrialization, Kyoto has 202 of the country's National Treasures (20 percent of the total) and 1,596 of its Important Cultural Assets (15 percent of the total).

Among these treasures from the past: Kyoto Imperial Palace, Nijo Castle, Katsura Detached Palace, Shugakuin Detached Palace, Nishi Honganji Temple, Higashi Honganji Temple, Kiyomizu Temple, Yasaka Shrine, Heian Shrine, and the beautiful Kinkakuji (Temple of the Golden Pavilion).

In addition to these historical treasures, Kyoto has three of the country's largest annual festivals (Gion, Heian and Aoi), along with a number of other major annual and monthly events that, combined, attract millions of visitors each year.

Kyoto is also the birthplace of No, Kyogen and Kabuki, and is the national center for *Chado* (the Tea Ceremony) and *Ikebana* (Flower Arranging), two of Japan's most important cultural practices.

While examples of Japan's traditional culture can be found in abundance throughout the islands, Kyoto has retained its role as the primary repository of the glories of old Japan, and no one can say they have "done Japan" without a visit to the ancient capital.

[27]
Playing the Geisha Game In Present-Day Japan

DURING THE 1600s in Edo (Tokyo) a special class of female entertainers who were skilled at playing the shamisen, singing, and dancing gradually came to be known as *geisha* (gay-ee-shah). *Gei* means art and *sha* means person.

The geisha performed for private individuals and parties in the country's large redlight districts, and in *ryokan* (rio-kahn) inns and *ryotei* (rio-tay-ee) restaurants. Because of their association with the courtesan quarters, and because prostitution was also commonly practiced in *ryokan* and *ryotei*, the geisha came to be regarded by many as a just another category of prostitutes.

However, as the decades of the Edo era (1603-1868) passed, the profession of the geisha grew in stature. Their training became more formalized and strict. Famous courtesans regularly hired geisha to help them entertain their high profile customers.

Although geisha did not work as prostitutes it became customary for them to form intimate liaisons with affluent men who patronized them regularly and treated them more or less as mistresses. Some geisha had more than one regular patron at the same time, but they were not for hire for indiscriminate sex, and having more than one patron simultaneous was frowned upon.

With the deterioration of the licensed gay quarters following the downfall of the Tokugawa Shogunate in 1867, the social status of prostitutes began to drop and that of the geisha to rise. Their training was expanded to include lessons in etiquette, grace, flower arranging, the tea ceremony, and in how to be stimulating conversationalists, making them among the most accomplished women in the country.

Within a few decades the position of prostitutes and geisha had completed reversed. Geisha were the most elite of public women, and prostitutes the lowest. Wealthy businessmen and high-ranking politicians began to vie with each other to make the most famous geisha their mistresses.

It was, in fact, common for men of wealth and power to marry their geisha mistresses, with one notable example being Hirobumi Ito (1841-1909), who played a key role in the overthrow of the Tokugawa Shogunate in the 1860s, became the chief architect of Japan's first constitution, and served as prime minister four times.

Given a social system in which wives did not participate directly or publicly with men in business or in politics, and therefore could not act as hostesses for their husbands under any circumstances, geisha came to perform valuable functions, not only dressing up business and political meetings held in *ryotei* inn restaurants but helping to make sure the meetings ran smoothly.

As late as the 1950s, Tokyo alone had over a dozen large so-called geisha districts, which consisted of clusters of *ryotei* that called in geisha nightly to serve their customers. Some *ryotei* had live-in geisha, but most of them lived in separate housing, and went to *ryotei* only when they were called. The services of the geisha were so costly that only wealthy businessmen and high-ranking politicians and government bureaucrats could afford to patronize them. [Their companies and agencies pay the bills as part of the entertainment budgets set aside for their managers and executives. Some managers in sales departments have huge budgets.]

Then the rapid transformation of Japan into an economic super power from the 1950s to the 1970s saw the equally rapid rise of thousands of cabarets and night clubs that featured hostesses as drinking, dancing and conversational companions, with fees far below what geisha inns charged.

The far less expensive cabarets and nightclubs attracted huge numbers of middle-class men from every walk of life, for business as well as personal reasons. During the heyday of this era, over half a million young women were employed as hostesses.

The more attractive the hostesses, and the more skilled they were in entertaining men, the more they could earn. This naturally attracted some of the most beautiful and socially talented young women in the country. Hundreds if not thousands of these remarkable women became millionaires. Like the geisha of an early day, many of them married well. One married the then president of Indonesia, Sukarno, and became an international celebrity.

The reign of the huge businessmen-oriented hostess cabarets and nightclubs ended in the late 1980s when Japan's economic bubble begin to deflate, but they were quickly replaced by dozens of thousands of dance clubs and other types of entertainment spots that catered to newly liberated, and affluent, female clientele as well as men.

The geisha survived the economic fallout, although they are now on the fringe of Japan's entertainment world. In Kyoto, in particular, there are well-known geisha districts, with many of the women in the trade being third and fourth generation geisha.

In the evenings in Tokyo's Akasaka district, which borders the country's government center, one can still see geisha being delivered to *ryotei* and *ryokan* in rickshaws pulled by men wearing traditional Edo age garb.

Most geisha now voluntarily enter the profession when they are in their late teens. Their training is less formal and less comprehensive, often as little as a few weeks, as opposed to years in earlier times.

But to the foreign resident or visitor, today's instant geisha are just as fascinating, just as entertaining, if not more so, than their predecessors. And they are almost always more attractive because today their popularity and success is more dependent upon their looks.

Few things are more satisfying than spending an evening in a *ryotei* restaurant in the company of geisha, participating in their games and experiencing a sensuous-charged atmosphere that has not changed for centuries.

[28]
The Influence of "Characters" On Japan's Culture

ONE OF THE elements that distinguishes Japanese culture, and is responsible for much of the country's exotic image as well as the mindset and special skills of the people, are the "characters" that make up the Japanese system of writing.

By "characters" we mean, of course, the Chinese ideograms with which the Japanese write the core words of their language. The Japanese term for the ideograms is *Kan ji* (Kahn-jee), usually written in Roman letters as one word (*Kanji*), which literally means "Chinese characters."

Kanji came into common use in China in the 14th century B.C., but it was not until the 3rd century A.D. that a scholar named Wani came to Japan from the ancient Korean kingdom of Kudara, bringing with him the Analects of Confucius, which were written in *Kanji*, and a textbook for studying the characters.

It was not until the 4th and 5th centuries A.D., however, that the use of *Kanji* began to spread in Japan, primarily via scholars and immigrants from kingdoms on the Korean Peninsula that had been under the suzerainty of China for many centuries.

As time passed Korean immigrants who were employed in Japan as official recorders gradually transcribed the whole Japanese language into *Kanji*.

By the 6th and 7th centuries, most male members of the elite class in Japan could read and write *Kanji*. Soon thereafter, scholars created two additional phonetic scripts (phonograms) to write portions of Japanese words that could not be rendered in Chinese characters.

During the early centuries following the adoption of *Kanji*, women were not allowed to study the ideograms, but many upper class women surreptitiously learned how to read and write with the newly developed phonetic scripts.

By the advent of modern times, the study and use of *Kanji* had become the foundation of all Japanese education, with an impact that went far beyond what one generally associates with a system of writing.

Leaning to read and draw—not <u>write</u>!—*Kanji* had a profound influence on the personality, character, aesthetic perceptions and physical dexterity of the Japanese.

Learning how to read the large number of *Kanji* used to write the language changed the way the Japanese looked at and reacted to the world around them because the *Kanji* represented both physical things and non-physical concepts – they were not just phonetic sounds like the English alphabet.

Learning how to draw the *Kanji* required all Japanese to become virtual artists, and this too changed their perceptions and attitudes. A significant percentage of the middle and upper class population went beyond drawing the *Kanji* in the "standard" form. They began stylizing the characters, turning their drawing into a fine art that came to be called *Shodo* (Show-doh), or "The Way of Writing," translated today as calligraphy.

Those who became especially skilled at *Shodo* were recognized and honored as master artists. How aesthetically attractive one could draw the *Kanji* became equated with morality and virtue.

Examples of *Shodo* by past masters are among the most treasured of Japan's historical artifacts. Today, most Japanese homes have at least one example of *Shodo* among their wall decorations.

To the untrained, casual eye, *Kanji* may appear to have neither rhyme nor reason, but familiarity with the characters reveals not only their pictorial meaning but their artistry as well.

In fact, it may be fair to say that in order to completely, fully, understand Japanese culture it is necessary to know *Kanji*. It is certainly true that many of the attributes of the Japanese that are positive and admirable owe much of their significance to the influence of *Kanji*.

In earlier times, to become fully literate the Japanese had to learn some 10,000 characters, requiring a much higher level of discipline and respect for teachers than our measly 26 letters—to say nothing of the time involved. Learning the some 2,000 characters required for literacy today remains a defining element in the character and mindset of the Japanese, and there are reflections of this discipline and respect in virtually everything they do.

Learning to recognize and interpret just a few dozen *Kanji* adds a valuable dimension to one's experience in Japan. And, of course, the more *Kanji* one knows the deeper and more gratifying the experience. Even if one is not motivated to learn and use *Kanji* as a means of communication, just viewing the characters as an art form adds grace to one's life.

Visitors to Japan often buy samples of Japanese Kanji calligraphy on scrolls to hang on walls in their homes as exotic decorative items.

[29]
Visitors Can Watch Svelte Female "Samurai"

IN JAPAN'S hundreds of *dōjōh* (dohh-johh), or martial arts gyms, throughout the country it is now common to see young women wielding wicked looking "swords" made of sheathes of bamboo, and shouting *ki* (kee) or some other sound at the top of their voices.

These young women say that they have taken up *kendō* (ken-dohh), or "the way of the sword," because it provides them with a direct connection with Japan's traditional culture, makes them feel "more Japanese," and fills a void in their lives.

This new phenomenon is being analyzed left and right by sociologists, psychologists and run-of-the-mill commentators, some of whom question the motives of the young women. One popular theme is that the women are not so much interested in regaining the spirit of the samurai as they are in "looking good" in skin-tight clothing as they cavort on the *dōjōh* floor.

Another explanation is that the young women find that practicing with a makeshift sword is an empowering experience because it allows them to demonstrate that they can become skilled in doing something that was traditionally seen as a male thing.

Practice in using swords was a major part of the lives of the warrior class that ruled Japan from 1192 until 1868, particularly male members, who were required to begin engaging in daily practice drills from the age of seven.

The samurai class was abolished in 1870 and the wearing of swords was banned shortly thereafter, but *kendō* itself did not disappear.* The military, the police and schools inaugurated *kendō* programs as a means of developing character and a fighting spirit.

In more recent decades the spirit of the samurai was kept alive in the public mind by kabuki, noh, movies, and long-running television serials. The appearance of the Tom Cruse film *The Last Samurai* in 2003 resulted in several old books on samurai becoming best sellers, including one that was published in 1716 and another one that was published in 1905.

Now there is a full-fledged *kendō* boom going on in Japan that is part of a revival of the samurai spirit, which provided the foundation of the traditional culture for many centuries.

There is no doubt that practicing *kendō* dramatically increases one's courage, self-confidence and outgoing spirit—something that most young Japanese girls of today already have in abundance without any *kendo* training.

Residents and visitors to Japan who would like to see some of these young women going through their *kendō* paces can catch the action at Tokyo's Shinjuku Sports Plaza dojo and the Iguchi Community Center in suburban Mitaka.

Kendō masters point out that the moves in this new "samurai exercise" are not the traditional moves of genuine sword fighters. They say it is an adaptation of the "art form" of sword fighting developed for kabuki, noh and the movies, in which there is no physical contact.

Physical contact or not, the girls look good! – making the *dōjōh* popular places on the itineraries of male visitors who are into martial arts.

[*See my books: *THE JAPANESE SAMAURAI CODE* and *SAMRAI STRAGEGIES* for insights into the mindset and behavior of this amazing class of people.]

[30]
Travelers Can Max Out On Japanese Manga

TRAVELERS in Japan who are *manga* (mahn-gah) fans can now max out on them by spending time in *manga-kissa* (mahn-gah kee-sah), or "manga cafés," that are stocked with hundreds of manga books that, for a small fee, patrons can sit and read for hours at a time.

For the few people around the world who are not familiar with the term *manga*, it refers to Japanese comic books, which, along with anime (ah-nee-may), the Japanese word for animated films, have taken the world by storm. Like kabuki, samurai and tsunami, these two words have transcended the Japanese language and become part of the vocabulary of the world.

Anime and manga have not only transcended international and linguistic borders, they have spawned two of the most dynamic industries in the world, and have become powerful cultural forces in Japan, in the U.S. and elsewhere.

Manga, or the comic books, generally come first because they provide the titles, names and storylines, and if they are successful they may be animated—a much more expensive process than printing and binding books.

Animation is, of course, a modern technology, but manga have been a part of Japanese life since the 7th century, when Buddhist monks began to create picture scrolls depicting animals, flowers, leaves and other symbols. Some of these early scrolls featured animals that acted like humans…and satirized Buddhist priests.

By the 13th century manga were being used to decorate the walls of temples. In the 16th century, manga began to appear as hanga (hahn-gah) or woodblock prints.

Some of the most popular of the larger of these prints depicted 69 different sexual positions, which, among other uses, were given to newly married couples on their wedding night.

In the 1700s manga woodblock print artists began to make collections of their prints, write captions for them, and bind them into books. By that time, the content of the prints ranged from exuberant eroticism and political satire to depictions of nature.

As the decades passed, artists began to include stories as well as captions in their manga books, with the narratives gradually becoming more and more important. Eventually, books illustrated with manga became the leading literary form in the country.

The most popular of these books featured prints and stories about famous courtesans in Japan's huge red-light districts, and were known as ukiyo-e (uu-kee-yoh-eh), which can be translated as "portraits of the floating world."

The word manga was created in 1815 by an artist named Hokusai, who was to become one of Japan's most famous hanga masters. He made the word up from ideograms meaning "whimsical" and "picture."

Just as Japan's woodblock prints had a major impact on European painters in the 16th and 17th centuries, Western techniques of shading, anatomy, and perspective were introduced into Japan in the late 1800s, resulting in dramatic changes in the appearance of manga.

By the early 1900s, manga books were a thriving part of Japan's new publishing industry. With the onset of war in the 1930s, the activities of manga artists and publishers came under government control. Only those that supported the military goals of the gov-ernment were allowed to stay in business, and then only on a drastically reduced scale.

With freedom restored in 1945 and the prewar publishing giants reduced to small operations, new manga artists and publishers sprang up by the hundreds, publishing cheap copies called akahon (ah-kah-hone) or "red books."

One of these new artists was a former medical student named Tezuka Osamu, who revolutionized the content of the comics by creating such characters as Mighty Atom and writing storylines in a variety of themes about real life. His New Treasure Island, published in 1947, sold over 400, 000 copies, resulting in the industry changing from producing comics for children to comics for teenager and adults.

Now, there are monthly manga for boys, for girls, for salary men, for young women, and for virtually every other group, covering everything from fashion and male-female relations to how to be an effective manager. The sales numbers of many of them are in the millions. A number of the most successful ones are sold around the world in translated editions.

Animated films based on Japanese manga are also sold world-wide, as theater films, television series and videos. Their plots run the gamut of human interests and emotions, from adventure and love stories to action films.

Their categories include mecha (may-chah), or "big robots;" hentai (hane-tie), or "porn;" martial arts, science fiction, fantasy, and "cyber punk," etc.

The Japan Foundation estimates that between 70 and 80 percent of the young people in the U.S. and other foreign countries now studying the Japanese language were influenced to do so by their desire to read manga in their original language.

[31]
Japan's Amazing Earthquake Technology

J APAN SITS on an earthquake belt that has resulted in some of the most destructive quakes in history, but in recent times no modern high-rise buildings have suffered any damage, attesting to their sophisticated quake-resistant construction.

In fact, Japan is noted for having the world's most advanced quake-resistant technology, and boasts over 500 buildings that are 100 or more meters high, none of which has ever lost as much as a window.

What is not generally known, however, is that the basis for this technology was discovered and was in use more than 1200 years ago.

Even more surprising, perhaps, is that the technology was first used in the construction of huge Buddhist temples and high-rise pagodas—a pagoda being, a many-storied Buddhist tower that originated in India, moved to China and Korea, and finally to Japan around 585 A.D.

Pagodas, built in the compounds of Buddhist temples, are both symbols of Buddhism and storage towers for sacred religious objects. The first pagodas in Japan were built entirely of wood, and had from three to five stories, topped by a spire that made them look even higher.

The 5-storied pagoda on the grounds of the Horyu Temple in Nara, built in the 6th century, undulates like a "snake dance" when an earthquake occurs, with the central pillar swinging like a long pendulum. The temple itself is believed to be the oldest wooden building in the world. The nearby Todai Temple, constructed between 724 and

749, is recognized as the largest wooden building in the world.

Both the Horyu and Todai temples and their adjoining pagodas have suffered some earthquake damage since they were built, but none have ever collapsed.

Architects and engineers who recently supervised repairs on the Toshodai Temple in Nara, built in 759, were well aware in advance that it had withstood many quakes in its 1,245-year history, but they were nevertheless amazed at the sophistication of the technology that made its survival possible.

The Takenaka Corporation engineer who supervised the repairs said that the temple construction consisted of wooden beam joints encircling huge pillars, which allowed the different parts of the building to shift slowly during an earthquake, absorbing the seismic vibrations.

He added that the joints of the large pillars supporting the tile roof of the huge temple absorbed the shock of earthquakes and allowed the pillars to tilt, but once the shaking was over the pillars returned to their upright position.

While various other types of earthquake-resistant technology have gone into the construction of high-rise buildings in Japan since the 1930s, the first building to make use of the ancient temple and pagoda technology was the 27-story, 130-meter-tall Umeda DT Tower in front of the JR Osaka Station, completed in 2003.

The new tower uses a hybrid, base-isolated, system combining three shock-absorbing devices between the second and third floors. The 30,000-ton weight of the building's upper floors is supported on 12 linear "riders." When an earthquake occurs, the upper portion of the building slides back-and-forth on shock absorbing devices, reducing the impact of the tremors by approximately 50 percent.

The Takenaka engineer said the difference between ancient Japanese builders and their Western counterparts illustrated a fundamental difference in Asian and Western philosophies.

He pointed out that early Westerners built "hard" unmoving structures of stone in an effort to resist the forces of nature, while Japanese buildings were constructed to absorb the energy of nature rather than resist it.

The huge Marunouchi Building in front of Tokyo Station, which opened in 2002, also uses shock absorbers to protect it from earth-quakes. Its dozens of shops and restaurants, the latter on its upper floors (with fantastic views of the Imperial Palace Grounds and central Tokyo), made it an instant tourist attraction.

Japan's advanced earthquake technology has made its high-rise buildings among the safest in the world. [For residents and visitors who are concerned about earthquakes, special "earthquake survival kits" are available from sporting goods stores. These kits include long ropes.]

[32]
"Just in Time" System Only Half of Story

BUSINESSMEN worldwide are now familiar with the Jaanese word *kanban* (kahn-bahn), which refers to a manufacturing system that helps eliminate waste, reduces cost, and ensures a higher level of quality than was previously possible in manufacturing processes.

What most of these business people are unaware of, however, is that the *kanban* process, pioneered by the predecessor of Toyota Motor Corporation (Toyoda Automatic Loom Works), was (and still is) only half of the equation that made it possible for Japanese manufacturers to surpass their American and European counterparts in both productivity and quality from around 1960 and on.

Kanban itself means a signboard, a billboard or poster, which the general manager of the Toyoda Loom Works began using (back in the early1930s) to list the parts needed on a minute-to-minute basis as products moved down an assembly line. This made it possible for suppliers to deliver the needed parts "just-in-time" to the assembly line workers.

In 1933 Toyoda Loom Works created an automobile division, spinning it off as an independent company, Toyota Motor Corporation, in 1937. [The difference in the name of the new company was an error in the choice of ideograms made by the person who registered the company.]

The *kanban* system, which had been significantly improved since first being introduced, became an integral part of Toyota Motor Corporation's manufacturing process.

Toyota describes the *kanban* system as an "information carrying device" and "a tool" for implementing the "pull" system of production, which puts parts on the line where they are needed, and immediately replaces the ones that are used.

Each kanban with its list of parts moves along the assembly line with the parts, so they reach the right place at exactly the right time.

The first successful post-World War II *kanban* aided automobile made by Toyota was the Toyopet Crown, introduced in 1955, and the rest, as the saying goes, is history.

But again it was not just the "just-in-time" system of delivering parts and information when and where they were actually needed that made Toyota, and subsequently hundreds of other Japanese corporations, so successful so quickly.

The other half of this equation, also created and spread by Toyota, was the principle and process of *jidoka* (jee-dohh-kah). *Jido* (jee-dohh) means "automatic, automatic motion, self-moving." *Ka* (kah) refers to something that is good, right, approved.

As used by Toyota, *jidoka* refers to building into automation the ability to detect and stop a malfunction (in the manufacturing process) before it occurs, and it was this technology that dramatically improved the ability of Japanese manufacturers to build products faster and cheaper and better in quality than foreign manufacturers.

The goal of *jidoka* is to prevent all defects, thereby ensuring that 100 percent quality is built into all products. When this process is coupled with the Japanese principle of *kaizen* (kigh-zen) or "continuous improvement," which has long been an integral part of the Japanese mind-set, it gives the Japanese a winning combination.

Not surprisingly, Korean manufacturers such as Samsung owe much of their own success to having integrated these two principles into their business culture. By the year

2000 Chinese manufacturers had begun striving to reach this stage—and they will get there, probably sooner than anyone expects.

It goes without saying (to use an old Japanese saying) that foreign manufacturers that have not yet picked up on the concept and use of *jidoka*, as well as *kaizen* [continuous improvement], are at a serious disadvantage, and may end up on the dust heap of history.

One of the most popular tours for foreign visitors in Japan is a visit to one or more Japanese factories where they can see how this remarkable system works. The differences between a Japanese factory and an American factory [making the same thing] is often startling.

In the 1970s, by which time Japan seemed to be on its way to colonizing the U.S., some American businessmen finally got the word and hordes of them began to flood Japan to see their factories—and some of them implemented what they learned when they came home.

[Hopefully, one of my books, *THE JAPANIZATION OF AMERICA*, (the Japanese edition: *Nihon-ka Suru Amerika*) had some influence on the sudden enlightenment of some if these people.]

[33]
Secrets of Japan's Award-Winning Designs

BETWEEN 1955 and 1970 the Japanese became world leaders in industrial and commercial design, a phenomenon that had a fundamental influence on American and European designers, making it imperative that they improve their own designs in order not to be totally replaced, as well as providing them with new insights into the nature of good design.

This phenomenon has a historical precedent. In the early 1600s foreigners in Japan began to ship various Japanese handicrafts to Europe wrapped in the now famous woodblock prints, which at the time were so cheap and so lightly regarded (at least by the foreigners) that they used them as wrapping paper.

In Europe the woodblock prints quickly became collector's items, changed hands for large sums of money, and dramatically influenced European painters in their use of form and color.

Long before that era, the Japanese sense of design had become an integral part of the culture. Rather than concentrating on philosophical quests for absolute or eternal truths, or occupy themselves with abstract concepts of a transcendental God or of art for art's sake, Japanese artists and designers endeavored to extract the essence of nature and then to express it in simplified as well as symbolic forms.

Instead of viewing straight and curving lines as opposing expressions, the Japanese regarded them as the same element in different manifestations, like water that is constantly undulating and changing its shape, or the flame of a candle that flickers, but both maintaining their essence.

For these reasons Japanese artists have traditionally avoided perfect symmetry in composition, believing that it lacked vitality.

Western industrial and commercial design concepts, introduced into Japan as early as the 1860s, were at first slavishly copied, and for nearly one hundred years the traditional Japanese sensibilities were suppressed by the Japanese themselves as well as by foreign importers who brought in their own product samples to be copied.

However, between 1945 and 1955 the Japanese sense of design, based on handicrafts and textiles that had achieved the level of fine arts more than a thousand years earlier, began to re-emerge and to reassert itself. Hundreds of design schools were established. Organizations began sponsoring design contests.

These ancient impulses were first applied to industrial machinery and again to textiles, and then gradually to products destined for the export market. The number of original product designs created in Japan between 1955 and 1965 was incredible to those who were not familiar with Japanese history.

In characteristic fashion, the Japanese expended enormous amounts of time, energy and talent on applying their traditional design sense to modern-day products, giving design a far higher priority than Western manufacturers were wont to do.

On the commercial/graphic design front, the Japanese did not have to go through a learning or adaptation process. As the economy grew from the 1950s on, so did the output and quality of graphic designs, particularly in posters, magazine and newspaper advertisements, and in book illustration.

A great deal of the sensual appeal and the overall ambiance of life in Japan today is a reflection or manifestation of the essence of Japanese design concepts in advertisements, architecture, automobiles, art, crafts, kimono, yukata, interior decorations, public posters, magazines, even in traditional food displays.

The power of Japanese design comes from the fact that it is a direct expression of both the dynamic and static aspects of nature, which has a positive impact on the human senses as well as the intellect and the spirit.

Foreigners wanting to do business in Japan can benefit enormously from studying and reflecting on the essence of Japanese design, and building it into their products and marketing programs.

All travelers need to do to reap the same benefit is to stop, look closely at things Japanese, open their minds, and let the natural energy flow into them.

[34]
In Japan Good Design is Everywhere!

IN THE 1960s and 70s a number of foreign scholars, Japan specialists and media pundits predicted that Japan would become the world's largest economy—bypassing and overshadowing the United States.

Those predictions were naïve to say the least, but Japan has in fact become a world leader in a number of key areas that include technological advances in several scientific fields, particularly the creation of new materials.

This development is especially remarkable because invention and innovation were virtually taboo in Japan from the mid-1600s until the last decades of the 19th century, putting the Japanese some 200 years behind the Western world in scientific research and technology.

But there is one area in which the Japanese have been more advanced than Westerners—intellectually as well as technologically—for well over a thousand years, and that is in the world of design and in the creation of arts and crafts that are superior in both design and quality.

As far back as the 7th century Korean immigrants began bringing sophisticated Chinese art and craft technology to Japan. During the golden Heian period (794-1185) this technology and the accompanying master/apprentice system of training were integrated into Japan's common culture.

Each generation of artists and craftsmen raised the bar on the standards of design and quality until they reached the level of a fine art. When the first Westerners showed up in Japan in the 16th century they were astounded at the technological ability of the Japanese and the quality of their crafts.

But it took the Japanese almost exactly one hundred years—from the 1860s to the 1960s—to get out from under the influence of foreign importers and to begin incorporating these traditional design and manufacturing skills into their export products, and the rest, as the saying goes, is history.

Today, the philosophical and ethical principles that are the foundation of Japanese design and product quality are being adopted worldwide, creating what is now being called a new era of design.

Despite the inroads that have been made in Japan by Westernization and modernization since the 1860s the traditional design and quality concepts are alive and well, and they are tangible and visible for all to see.

Even in crowded Tokyo and other Japanese cities the evidence of good design and quality are visible on subways and trains and in the streets—on advertising posters, on storefronts, in product displays, in the architecture and interior furnishings of shops and restaurants, in buildings and offices.

For the discerning foreign visitor in Japan, just a few days can be an extraordinary aesthetic and cultural experience that is the highlight of the trip. If you look closely, the whole country is a virtual museum of modern and traditional art that adds an emotional, intellectual and spiritual ambiance to daily life.

[35]
Look Out Bill and Steve! Here Come Kohei and Genri!

Until the late 19th century you could count the number of Japanese entrepreneurs on a few hands and feet. People just didn't start new businesses, either because there were no new ideas or starting a new business was prohibited by the government and/or by deeply entrenched custom.

In fact, it was not until the last decades of the 20th century that entrepreneurship began to attract public attention in Japan. Up to that time high school and university graduates went directly from school to work for some company—and the bigger and more famous the company the better because they offered lifetime employment.

The 1990-1 "Big Bang" in reverse that let much of the air out of Japan's "bubble economy" resulted in a new mentality of individualism and personal independence among a growing number of young Japanese, changing things dramatically.

Now, hundreds of thousands of young Japanese prefer to work part-time or on a contract basis rather than as full-time regular employees, and thousands of them have done what was unthinkable just a short while ago—they have founded their own companies.

What is even more extraordinary—for Japan—is that many of these new entrepreneurs start their businesses before they finish school. In some cases, while they are still in high school, without bothering to go on to college.

Said one successful 20-year-old company president of a research firm that comes up with new product ideas: "Academics have no bearing on business."

He started his company with several of his buddies when they were still in high school. One of their first clients was the cosmetics giant Kanebo.

Another facet of this extraordinary phenomenon in Japan involves a growing number of young men and women who have taken an entirely new look at such traditional materials as silk, wood and hand-made paper, and are creating new products that combine modern and futuristic designs with the innate aesthetic qualities of the materials they use.

Kyoto, the Imperial capital of Japan from 794 until 1868 and the center of Japan's arts and crafts for more than a thousand years, has become a hotbed of entrepreneurship in the creation of new apparel and furniture lines. By 2000 this new breed of businessmen and women had reached the point that they were exhibiting and selling in New York, Milan and other global markets.

Young female entrepreneurs are among the leaders in this movement, working with traditional silk producers and dyeing companies to create handbags, jackets, and other apparel that are unique not only in their materials but in the artistry of their designs.

The day has obviously arrived when younger Japanese are going back to their cultural traditions as a source of creative ideas that can be turned into modern-day products—tapping into handicraft traditions that achieved the level of fine arts more than a thousand years ago.

This new breed of Japanese fashion designers, with their access to classic materials and unique Oriental design concepts, could very well eclipse the pop designers of Milan, New York and Paris in the near future.

It is surely this new breed of Japanese that holds the future of Japan in their hands. No longer chained to the past, no longer prohibited from using their imagination, and now having access to totally new frontiers of opportunity, they could take Japan to a new level.

AMAZING JAPAN – 119

One famous Kyoto manufacturer of incense now sells his products worldwide, achieving the sweet smell of success from a strictly domestic product that was once seen mostly in shrines and temples and at funerals.

[36]
Live Long & Prosper In Japan's "Shangri La"

THERE IS A kind of "Shangri La" in Japan that is not isolated by high mountains and frigid weather. In fact, it is more tropical than temperate, and you can wear skimpy clothing and go swimming in the sea the year-around.

This land of sunshine and clear blue water consists of a string of some 60 islands stretching around 800 miles between Kyushu (Japan's southernmost main island) and Taiwan. These islands make up Okinawa Prefecture—with Okinawa island being the largest in the group and the business, cultural, and economic center.

An independent kingdom for most of its history (which goes back at least 32,000 years), Okinawa was invaded and captured by the Shimazu fiefdom on southern Kyushu in 1609, but it was not formally merged into the Japanese empire until the 1870s.

In the summer of 1945 Okinawa was invaded and captured by American and Allied forces during the last days of World War II (known in Japan as the Pacific War), and has since done double duty as a site for U.S. military bases.

All of the Okinawan islands were administered by the U.S. military from 1945 to 1972, when they were returned to Japan. Now, growing as a business bridge between Japan, Taiwan, China and Southeast Asia, Okinawa has also become a major tourist destination.

In addition to its distinctive part-Southeast Asian and part-Japanese culture, along with its historical artifacts and tropical oceanic atmosphere (with the East China Sea on its east side and the Pacific Ocean on its west side), Okinawa is particularly renowned for the longevity of its people.

In fact, it is generally recognized that the older generation of Okinawan men and women live longer on average than any another other group of people on the globe. The reason for this, the experts say, is both cultural and dietary.

Most older Okinawans have clung to their traditional lifestyle—working outside the year around as farmers, craftsmen and fishermen, engaging in recreational activeties such as folk dancing, and otherwise remaining active from sun up to sun down.

But the primary key to their extraordinary longevity is attributed to their diet—which is becoming increasingly famous around the world as a result of a flood of Okinawa diet books, magazine and newspaper articles, and the preaching of television health gurus.

Not surprisingly, the incidence of cancer, heart diseases and other maladies that afflict older people is far lower in Okinawa than anywhere else in the world. Most Okinawans die of old age when they are in their 80s, 90s and 100s without ever having suffered a serious illness.

These older Okinawans do not stint on their eating. Volume-wise, they eat as much if not more than most other people. It's what they eat that counts. Their diet consists mostly of vegetables and grains that have about half of the calories per gram of food as the typical American and European diets.

Says a health researcher: "They eat a diet high in carbohydrates, but they are good carbs—not things that cause a rapid rise in blood sugar."

High on the list of things Okinawans eat: vegetables, sweet potatoes, whole grains, fruit, soy foods, beans, seafood, seaweed, konnyaku (a vegetable jelly) yogurt and lean meat. And they use a lot of Southeast Asian spices, resulting in their diet sometimes being referred to as "Japanese food with salsa."

Older Okinawans follow three basic principles in their eating: *kuten gwa* (eating small portions), *hara hachi-bu* (stop eating when you are 80 percent full), and *nuchi gusui* (eating with the idea that food has healing power). And they eat few if any processed foods.

The Okinawan diet is gradually making inroads into mainland Japan, with Okinawa restaurants springing up all over. Tokyoites and foreign visitors can now experience traditional Okinawan dishes at more than a dozen restaurants.

Among them: Miyarabi in Ikebukuro's Ark City (building), which features cuisine based on ancient royal palace recipes and live entertainment; and Narabi to Kanado, which has two branches in Shinjuku, one in the Isetan Kaikan (next to the famous Isetan Department Store), and the other in the My City building adjoining Shinjuku Station.

[37]
Japan's Martial Arts Build Self-Confidence, Courage

MARTIAL ARTS are now inseparably linked with Japan even though there are martial arts traditions in many other countries.

Kung Fu is of Chinese origin. Taekwondo (Tie-kwan-doh) is Korean. Karate (Kah-rah-tay), originally from China, was developed in Okinawa when that island was an independent kingdom, had its own language and culture, and regarded Japan as an enemy.

Stick-fighting was long a national art in Indonesia, and, of course, sword-fighting and the use of the bow had long traditions in Europe and other parts of the world.

Not only were the martial arts highly developed in China and Korea long before they became known in Japan, both China and Korea had classes of professional fighting men centuries before the appearance of Japan's famous samurai warriors.

But it was, in fact, the appearance of the samurai in the 12th and 13th centuries A.D. as Japan's ruling class that resulted in martial arts becoming a key factor in the lives of the Japanese. Samurai, literally "one who serves," not only enforced the laws of Japan's Shogunate government, they also became the administrators on every level of government.

Training in martial arts and extraordinarily strict discipline was the keystone of the education of all male members of samurai families. While less intense, females in the samurai class were also trained in a highly stylized and strict form of behavior, and for some, this training included the use of weapons.

Thus, over generations, martial arts became institutionalized and even ritualized in Japan's ruling class, and the fact that the samurai prevailed in Japan until the latter part of the 19th century resulted in the arts surviving into modern times.

During Japan's long Shogunate era (1185-1867), the most notorious of the country's martial arts practitioners were the *ninja* (neen-jah), or "stealers in"—men and women in certain clans who were trained from childhood to be assassins, secret agents and terrorists, and were for hire.

After the fall of the feudal Shogunate government in Japan in 1867, training in martial arts became even more widespread because it was no longer the exclusive preserve of the country's upper class. The military forces, police forces, and both public and private schools conducted training in martial arts.

But following the downfall of the Shogunate system of government in 1867, a number of private individuals, not connected with the military or government, began to transform Japan's most popular martial arts—aikido, judo, karate and kendo—into sports, aimed at developing healthy bodies and disciplined, moral minds.

With the transformation of Japan itself into a nation dedicated to peace at the end of World War II, the new versions of the martial arts quickly came into their own as sports. Movies, international tournaments and the Olympics exposed Japan's martial arts to the world, making them the country's most popular cultural export.

There are now thousands of *dojoh* (doh-joh), or martial arts gyms, around the world. Thousands of Y's and schools also have martial arts programs. All of them teach not only the physical side of the arts but the ethical and moral side as well—something that is sorely lacking in many public educational systems.

Parents should not be turned off by the term "martial arts," which may suggest fighting and violence to those who are not familiar with the changes that have occurred in since the mid-1900s.

All of the main arts—aikido, judo, karate and kendo—are now true sports, and parents who would like to give their children a good grounding in self-confidence, discipline and moral behavior would do well to enroll them in a martial arts program.

Of the four arts named above, kendo is the least known and least practiced outside of Japan, but it is one of the best of the arts for teaching courage, perseverance, and a disciplined lifestyle, for adults as well as children and for women as well as men.

And it is great for relieving stress—which contributes to mental and physical health.

See my book: *Samurai Principles & Practices that Will Help Preteens & Teens in School, Sports, Social Activities & Choosing Careers.* It provides the foundation for instilling the most desirable and admirable character traits in young people.

[38]
The Story Behind Japan's Notorious Ninja

OVER THE AGES virtually all larger countries have had their cadres of spies and secret agents who carried out undercover activities, from assassinations to sabotage, against their enemies and competitors, real and imagined.

But until recent times no country had spies and secret agents who were as well trained, as versatile, or as deadly, as Japan's infamous *ninja* (neen-jah) who, according to historical records, made Great Britain's fictitious James Bond come off looking like an over-age boy scout.

The term *ninja* has become known around the world as a result of movies and books and the growing international popularity of martial arts such as *karate* (kah-rah-tay) and *aikido* (aye-kee-doh)—but few people know the full story of Old Japan's secret agents.

The *ninja* of pre-modern Japan practiced the art of *ninjutsu* (neen-jute-sue)—which is sometimes translated as "the art of invisibility" or "stealing in"—and used a variety of weapons and implements that would make today's high-tech oriented spooks proud.

Historical records indicate that the first *ninja* were trained by Otomo no Hosoto, a famous warrior from Omi Province in the service of Prince Shotoku (574-622 A.D.), who served as the Regent for Empress Suiko.

Otomo devised special tactics used by secret agents in his employ who were dispatched on missions to spy on the Prince's enemies, steal documents, and commit other acts designed to weaken or destroy them.

Two types of *ninjutsu* strategies were developed: *yohjutsu* (yohh-jute-sue) or overt practices, and *injutsu* (een-jute-sue) or covert practices. *Yohjutsu* was used to infiltrate enemy ranks using disguises and assumed identities. *Injutsu* was a method of entering into places without being seen—at which the *ninja* became so clever the general populace believed they could make themselves invisible.

When engaged in an *injutsu* mission the *ninja* worked at night, and wore black apparel and hoods that left only a narrow slit for their eyes. The *ninja* uniforms had numerous secret pockets where they carried their weapons and the tools of their trade, which allowed them to scale vertical walls, bore holes in wood or the ground, saw through walls, swim long distances underwater, blow up buildings using gunpowder, and deal with large numbers of well-armed warriors.

The heyday of the *ninja* were the 101 years of the Sengoku period (1467-1568), when rival clan warlords fought to gain control of the country. Samurai warriors from Iga Province (now Mie Prefecture) and the Koga region of Omi established secret camps where large num-bers of *ninja* were trained from childhood.

The techniques these two groups taught came to be known as the Iga and Koga schools of *ninjutsu*, and are credited with spawning other schools that were to follow. The so-called Iga and Koga schools actually consisted of 49 extended families whose members lived in isolated mountain camps, and were all trained in *ninjutsu* as the family profession.

The training in *ninjutsu* was rigorous and comprehensive. It included running, jumping, climbing, swimming, the use of weapons and disguises, studying geography, topography, astronomy and history, learning to distinguish and imitate the sounds of animals and birds, learning local dialects, learning how to make and dispense poisons, and so on. *Ninja* were also taught to endure heat, cold, hunger, pain, and other discomforts.

Throughout Japan's early history, *ninja,* both males and females who were masters at playing the role of priests, traveling salesmen, entertainers, and other ordinary people commonly seen on the road were employed by the shoguns, by provincial lords, and by local authorities.

Ninja were especially clever at avoiding capture, but when all of their abilities and ruses failed, they could expect to be subjected to the severest torture in an attempt to find out who hired them. If capture became unavoidable, suicide was often the preferred choice.

One of the ways used to test people suspected of being *ninja* was to suddenly put them in extreme danger to see how they reacted. If a person leaped several feet aside to escape a falling object or jumped to the top of a high fence, in a split second, their cover was blown.

Real, live *ninja* can still be seen today at the *Nikko Edo Mura* (Nikko Edo Village) theme park near the mountain town of Nikko, famed as one of the most scenic spots in Japan, and the site of Shogun Ieyasu Tokugawa's spectacular mausoleum.

The *ninja* reenact a variety of *ninjutsu* techniques and skills that made them one of the world's deadliest and most feared societies of secret agents.

In one of the most extraordinary assassinations on record a ninja secreted himself in the toilet pit beneath the floor of the target's home. When the victim came in and squatted down over the opening of the pit to defecate the ninja impaled him with a short spear.

[39]
A Japanese Custom Worth Emulating

ONE OF THE most enviable facets of life in Japan is the fact that several million present-day Japanese (some say as many as 10 million or more) regularly write *haiku* (high-kuu) poetry.

Haiku readings and contests abound, including an annual national event that is sponsored by the emperor and empress at the Imperial Palace. One of the greatest honors a Japanese poet can aspire to is an invitation to attend one of the palace poetry celebrations.

Poetry has played an important role in Japanese life from prehistoric times. As in most ancient cultures, the early Japanese used verbal chants and songs that were essentially poetry to commune with nature and the gods. When they adapted the Chinese system of writing to their language between 400 and 600 A.D. their chants, songs and poetry were among the first things to be transcribed into the Chinese ideograms.

In the beginning, Japanese scholars, Buddhist monks and others imitated the poetic forms that were imported from China with the ideographic system of writing. But over the generations, the character of the Japanese language and the cultural penchant of the Japanese to standardize everything they did resulted in the creation of the form that became the *haiku* that is known today.

Japan's famous samurai warriors, who ruled the country from 1192 until 1868, were often as renowned for their ability to compose *haiku* as for their skill in swordsmanship.

In fact, until the changes wrought by mass industrialization and the importation of Western culture from 1945 on, it was almost *mandatory* that all Japanese write *haiku*. It was simply a part of their psyche…an expression of their Japanese identity.

It is because of the existence of a precise, unvarying form for *haiku* and a cultural compulsion that goes back for thousands of years that so many Japanese today continue to write *haiku*, and why it plays such an important role in their intellectual and spiritual life.

The dedicated 5-7-5-syllable form removes all challenges from structuring a *haiku* poem. *Haiku* magazines frequently carry articles about the "limitless power of the fixed form," pointing out that anyone can compose a poem simply by filling in the seventeen syllables.

Others say that writing and enjoying *haiku* provides a common link for the Japanese to communicate with each other across generational gaps in a society that has become so complex that people tend to wall themselves off from each other.

One of the attractions of *haiku* poetry is that its meanings or messages can be interpreted in more than one way, and this interpretation generally depends upon the sensibilities and intellectual prowess of the individual reading it. Another element of *haiku* poetry is that it is written for the benefit of the writer. As long as its message is clear to the author, he or she reaps its full benefit.

In addition to hundreds of private haiku clubs throughout Japan, schools on all levels sponsor *haiku* events, and many cafes and coffee shops provide venues for *haiku* readings.

Haiku has become one of Japan's most successful cultural exports, with hundreds of thousands of people worldwide not only enjoying translations of Japanese *haiku*, but also writing their own poems in English and other languages.

The set form and traditions of *haiku* provide a unique way for ordinary people of all ages to enjoy and benefit from the power of poetry. The Japanese practice of writing *haiku* as a universal cultural expression is a custom worth emulating.

Probably the most famous haiku ever written is this classic by Matsuo Basho [1644-1694]:

古池や
蛙飛込む
水の音

furuike ya
kawazu tobikomu
mizu no oto

[My translation]:

An old pond
A frog leaps in
The sound of water

[40]
Amazing Ainu – The "Indians" of Japan

LONG BEFORE the coming of the Japanese to the islands now known as Japan, the northern portion of the island chain was inhabited by tribes of ancient people whose physical traits were not typically Oriental.

These tribes inhabited the northern part of the main island of Honshu, all of Hokkaido, the Kurile islands and the southern portion of Kamchatka Peninsula, and in that sense they were the indigenous "Indian" tribes of these regions.

These first inhabitants of Japan called themselves *Ainu* (Aye-nuu), which means human or man—and is similar to the custom of some of the Indian tribes of North America, the Navajo in particular, who call themselves *Diné* (Din-eh) or "The People."

Unlike the indigenous Indian tribes of North and South America, however, the *Ainu* inhabitants of Japan had physical features that made them distinctly different from Oriental Asians as well as the Indians of the Americas.

The eyes of the *Ainu* did not have the epicanthic fold that is characteristic of Orientals. Their eyes were unusually large and round, even for Caucasians, and ranged from brown, light brown and gray, to blue-gray. Also unlike Orientals and American Indians, *Ainu* men had exceptionally heavy body and facial hair.

The earliest mention of the *Ainu* of Japan and the regions north of Japan is found in ancient Chinese records, which refer to them as "the hairy people."

It seems that the *Ainu* originated somewhere on the northeastern Asian continent (like the original, indigenous tribes of Korea who disappeared long ago), and then moved southward over eons of time.

In contrast, the ancestors of modern Japanese came from Korea, China and the islands that extend southwest to Taiwan. As these newcomers moved northward on the island chain they began encountering the *Ainu* just north of what is now Tokyo.

The new Asian immigrants to Japan were more culturally advanced than the native *Ainu*, considered them sub-human, both racially and culturally, and presumed that they had no rights to the areas they inhabited—just as European Americans were to view and treat indigenous American Indians in more modern times.

By the 7th century A.D., the Japanese were launching major military campaigns against the *Ainu*, decimating their population and pushing those who survived further north. This was the period when the term *shogun* (show-goon) first came into use in the compound *Sei-i-Tai Shogun*, which translates as "Barbarian Subduing General," used to designate generals charged with eliminating the *Ainu*.

Large numbers of *Ainu*, like American Indians in later centuries, also died from diseases that were new to them.

By the 19th century there were only twenty to thirty thousand *Ainu* left. A few of these survivors lived in still relatively isolated mountainous regions north of Tokyo, and the rest in Hokkaido and on the Kurile islands north of Hokkaido.

It was during this era that the Japanese government, on the advice of an American politician, resolved to eliminate the *Ainu* as a distinctive culture by forbidding the use of the *Ainu* language, forcing the *Ainu* to take Japanese names, and prohibiting the practice of their traditional customs.

The attempt to eradicate *Ainu* culture ended in the 20th century, and by the last decades of the century there was a growing movement among the remaining population to revive their language and many of their cultural ways. However, racial mixing has continued to diminish the number of full-blooded *Ainu*, and they now number only a few thousand, most of who live in small villages in Hokkaido, Japan's northernmost island.

Ainu-Japanese mixtures are especially conspicuous in the vicinity of Sendai, north of Tokyo. They are noticeable for their abundant hair, and for their eyes. Strangely, the genes that make the *Ainu* eye are often incompatible with the genes of the Japanese eye, making deformities common. The most common of these deformities is eyes that are too far apart; often to such an extreme that one of the eyes withers away.

But, when the two sets of eye genes work, especially in females, the results are astounding. Their eyes are huge, striking in color, and so hypnotic that people can't avoid staring at them. In the 1950s and 60s, a number of mix-blood Ainu-Japanese girls were brought to Tokyo from the Sendai area and put to work as models and as extras in movies.

They were very successful as models—giving rise to the Japanese art and comic preference for drawing young females with huge, luminous eyes—but they did not fare as well as movie starlets because their eyes distracted so much attention from the Japanese stars.

Visiting one or more of the remaining *Ainu* villages in Hokkaido is like stepping through a time portal to an age when the world was young.

[41]
KARAOKE!
(Kah-rah-oh-kay)
Somebody Really Invented It!

MOST PEOPLE who have sung and heard karaoke probably believe it was something that grew of its own accord, like crab grass! But that is not the case. It was invented...by a guy who could not possible have dreamed that it would spread around the world like some kind of Asian flu.

Singing in Japan goes back to ancient times, when it became an integral part of Japanese culture. It began with shamans and priests chanting their ritual prayers to the gods.

Then fishermen, boatmen, carpenters, geisha, samurai warriors, shoguns, cooks, you name it, got into the act. Everybody sang—in groups and individually—to enhance work camaraderie, for self-gratification, as well as to entertain others.

Virtually every category of personal and public activity had its own collection of songs. The practice of singing became such an important part of Japanese culture that it survived into modern times.

Still today, singing is a significant part of the business and social life of the Japanese. It is perfectly common for reserved, elderly businessmen and politicians to burst out in song at public events—something that generally surprises—and invokes envy—from their Western counterparts.

And it was because of this imperative that everyone sing—for both business and pleasure and to relieve stress and bond with co-workers and new friends—that Daisuke Inoue invented karaoke.

In 1970 Daisuke Inoue was a club musician who earned his keep by playing sing-along tunes in cabarets in Kobe, Japan. It was painfully obvious to Daisuke that many of his businessmen "customers" had been so consumed by work that unlike other Japanese they had never had time to polish their singing skills.

This prompted Daisuke to tape a number of the more popular tunes (like Frank Sinatra's "I Did It My Way!"), changing the pitches to suit off-key singers, and making it possible for the cabaret customers to sing along with the taped tunes and not sound like screeching banshees.

Over the next several months, Daisuke integrated the "singer friendly" tunes into a tape recorder that became the first *karaoke* (kah-rah-oh-kay) machine that played only accompaniments. *Kara* (kah-rah) means empty and *oke* (oh-kay) is the Japanese abbreviation of orchestra. In other words, "empty orchestra."

In 1971 Daisuke made 12 karaoke machines and leased them to bars in Kobe. And as the saying goes, the rest is history…but not the kind of history most inventors dream of.

Following the incredible success of his first karaoke machines, Daisuke's intuition and ingenuity failed him. He didn't patent the new device, and before you could say *Dohshimashita ka?* (doh-she-mah-ssh-tah kah?)—which you might translate as "What the Hell happened!"—a whole stream of karaoke machines poured into Japan's huge number of bars and cabarets.

The new device was so popular that thousands of new "karaoke bars" were opened to take advantage of it. Hotels and other public buildings in the country opened "karaoke rooms" for their guests and employees.

Major manufacturers got into the act, using the latest technology to continuously upgrade the quality of karaoke machines. By the late 1980s karaoke had spread around the world, and went on to become one of Japan's most popular exports.

In 1999 *Time* magazine named Daisuke Inoue one of the 20 most influential Asians of the Century, along with China's Mao Tse-tung and India's Gandhi. I don't remember the *Time* piece, but naming the inventor of the karaoke machine in the company of such luminaries was surely not a tongue-in-cheek thing.

In 2004 Harvard University students awarded Daiskuke one of their annual Ig Nobel Prizes for contributing to world piece though his invention...the Ig being short for ignoble, and the annual Ig Nobel Prize is a parody of the real Nobel Prize.

Daisuke was invited to Harvard to receive the award in person, and sang a song before an appreciative audience. He was awarded the Ig Noble Prize for Peace for the contributions his invention made to world harmony.

This belated recognition is all that Daisuke's gets from his innovative invention. He could not compete with the big companies that jumped into manufacturing and marketing karaoke machines. His business failed. The last time I heard he lived in Nishinomiya, just outside of Kobe, and sold rat repellant devices.

Some of the millions of people around the world who have had their peace and quiet disturbed by home karaoke singing may wish that Daisuke had come up with his rat repellant business first.

[42]
Japan's Guest House is a Sight to See!

THE PALACES of Japan's emperor and empress and the princes and princesses—ensconced behind moats, ancient walls, the lay of the land and thick foliage—are hidden from all except for aerial views... and on New Year's Day.

But there is one "palace" that is not only out in the open, it is one of the most impressive sights in Tokyo, and yet very few visitors get more than a tantalizing glimpse of it as they drive by its spacious grounds.

This is the stately *Geihinkan* (Gay-ee-heen-kahn) or State Guest House, which was originally the Togu (Toh-guu) Palace, built during the first years of the Meiji Era (1868-1912).

In 1872 the Togu Palace was renamed the Akasaka Detached Palace. In 1873, when the Imperial Palace buildings burned down, it became the temporary residence of Emperor Meiji. Some years later it was used as the official residence of the Crown Prince, who became Emperor Taisho in 1912.

Patterned after the Versailles Palace of France, the Geihinkan was designed by Tokuma Katayama, a Japanese architect who studied under England's famous Josiah Condor and was one of the first Japanese architects to design a Western style building.

The present structure, completed in 1909, stands in grounds covering an area of 117,000 square meters and is built in French neo-baroque style, with a patina-green roof and granite facades.

From 1912 until 1972 the Detached Palace served as a site for ministerial meetings. A portion of it was also used as the National Diet Library, and in the early 1960s it became an office for the organizers of the 1964 Tokyo Olympics.

Following the Olympics, the palace underwent major renovation and was reopened in 1974 as the State Guest House.

To say that the Geihinkan is grand and opulent does not do justice to it. It is lavishly furnished with thick carpeting, elegant furniture, decorative tiles, ceiling murals that include a depiction of scenes from Noh plays, and a huge one-of-a-kind chandelier in the main hall.

The huge Guest House compound is on the southwest side of the Imperial Palace grounds, just outside what was once a palace moat and is now the bed for a commuter train line. It is a 7-minute walk form Yotsuya Station, where the JR Chuo and Sobu train lines and the Marunouchi and Namboku subway lines intersect.

Numerous kings, presidents, prime ministers and other notables, including Lady Diana, have stayed at the Geihinkan. It is also used as a banquet hall for entertaining dignitaries, and as a place to sign international treaties.

It is open to the public only a few days out of the year, and entrance is reserved for those lucky enough to win an annual drawing, which is held well in advance of the day.

Geihinkan by itself just means "guest house," and there are commercial geihinkan in many Japanese cities. The State Guest House is known publicly as *Akasaka no Geihinkan* (Ah-kah-sah-kah no Gay-ee-heen-kahn), or "The Akasaka Guest House," and that is the name you should use if going there by taxi.

[43]
Japan is Number One For Street Strolling

BANGKOK, Hong Kong, Kula Lumpur, Singapore, Seoul and a number of cities in China have areas that attract strollers, and many Western cities from New Orleans and Paris to Casa Blanca are equally well known for their strolling districts.

But few cities anywhere in the world compare with Tokyo, Kyoto, Osaka, Kobe, and hundreds of other cities throughout Japan in the number and variety of districts and streets that are meccas for strollers.

Strolling in the streets in the evenings and on weekends and holidays has been a common practice in Japan for at least a thousand years, but it was to become an institutionalized—and virtually ritualized—practice during the Tokugawa Shogunate, which began in 1603.

During the last two centuries of this period the Japanese strolled not only the streets of the cities, they strolled the highways of the country [there were few wheeled transportation devices on the roads], going on walks that lasted from weeks to months.

The rationale of some of these long walks was to visit shrines and temples around the country. Others did it just for the experience.

Among Japan's most famous walkers was the great haiku poet Basho, and the already mentioned fictionalized Yajiro and Kitahachi, two residents of Yedo, the Shogunate capital, who did it to get away from carping wives and have fun on the road. [Virtually all inns had good-time girls available for male travelers, so you can see why traveling was so popular among men.]

Other people who were constantly on the road during the Tokugawa era were *ronin* (roh-neen) or masterless samurai, gamblers, sumo wrestlers, and fief lords with retinues of servants and warriors. When the Lord of the Maeda fief went to Yedo (Tokyo) every other year to take his turn at the Shogun's Court he traveled with approximately 1,000 retainers.

In the late 1800s the paving of the main street in Tokyo's Ginza district and the construction of gas lights along the street resulted in it becoming the top strolling area in the country. *Ginbura* (Geen-buu-rah), or "Strolling the Ginza," became virtually mandatory for every resident and visitor in the city—a custom that continues today.

But the Ginza now has competition as the most popular strolling area in the city and in the country—not from just a few places but from thousands. In Tokyo alone there are several hundred districts that regularly attract huge numbers of strollers.

Among these hundreds, the largest and most popular include Asakusa, Akasaka, Akihabara, Aoyama, Harajuku, Hibiya, Ikebukuro, Kabukicho, Odaiba, Omotesando, Roppongi, Shibuya, Shinjuku, Ueno, and Yurakucho.

Every town and city in Japan has its large and small shopping and entertainment districts that regularly attract hundreds to hundreds of thousands of strollers.

Large cities like Yokohama (with its China Town), Nagoya, Kyoto, Osaka, Nagasaki, Hiroshima and Kagoshima, not to mention Sendai, Aomori and Sapporo, have from dozens to hundreds of districts that attract strollers.

Strolling districts in Osaka rival those in Tokyo, with Shinsaibashi and Tenjinbashi, being two of the largest and most famous—and in the eyes of many, both are far more colorful and fascinating than their counterparts in Tokyo.

Visitors to Japan should put strolling high on their list of things to do.

[44]
Japan Remains Safe Haven For Foreign Travelers

JAPANESE WHO travel abroad are repeatedly warned in travel literature, by their travel agents, by friends, and by the news media that once they leave Japan they will be in danger of being robbed, injured or even killed if they do not remain alert and take special measures to protect themselves.

The Japanese are cautioned never to set their bags down in a hotel lobby or in any kind of transportation terminal; to never walk in certain areas of cities at night; to be wary of conmen, touts, and so on.

Unfortunately, these warnings are not exaggerated or based on unwarranted fears. Given the number of Japanese who are robbed and often beaten while they are abroad it is remarkable that so many—some 14 to 15 million—continue to travel overseas each year.

In contrast to this, it is so rare for a foreign traveler in Japan to be robbed, beaten, killed or even harassed in any way that when it does happen it makes national headlines.

The incidence of violent crimes has gone up dramatically in Japan since the introduction of democracy and Western culture following the end of World War II in 1945, but the crime rate is still far below that of Western countries, and generally does not involve foreign victims.

One often hears that in Japan women can walk alone, at all hours of the night, in city districts that are notorious for their low life and the presence of street thugs and professional gangsters without fear of being accosted, robbed or raped. And that is true.

One also hears that *foreign* women are even safer when they are out and about in Japan—wherever they may be and whatever the hour—because Japanese males, including the criminal element, are less likely to harm foreigners. And that is true.

The continuing low level of crime in Japan, in particular the low incidence of people being attacked in the streets—day or night—can be attributed to Shinto and Buddhist standards established in the culture very early in Japan's history, and reinforced politically and socially during the long Shogunate period (1185-1868), when armed samurai warriors administered the country and were empowered to severely punish law and custom breakers.

During the early decades of the Tokugawa Shogunate (1603-1867), samurai warriors were legally permitted to kill people on the spot for violations of etiquette or the law that today would be consider minor infractions.

Given the combined influence of Shintoism and Buddhism, both of which advocated non-violence, and the social morality mandated and enforced by the samurai rulers of Japan, ordinary Japanese became paragons of honesty and good manners.

Still today, people routinely leave unlocked bicycles on the sidewalks and in front of stores and stations. As a rule, you can leave a bag or some other possession virtually anywhere in public and it will be there when you get back. Shops routinely put product displays outside, and leave them unguarded.

It is said that the extraordinary success of vending machine marketing in Japan occurred because it was possible to set them up out in the open, unprotected places, with virtually no chance that they would be vandalized and robbed.

Stories abound of the time and effort people expend to return lost or forgotten property, especially where foreign travelers are concerned. This is not only a manifestation of the honesty that is built into the character of the Japanese. It is also because the Japanese feel that they and the whole country are responsible for the welfare of visitors.

This security factor is one of Japan's greatest assets, and is an integral part of the attraction that the country has a travel destination. It is also one of the reasons why foreign residents are so attracted to life in Japan.

[45]
Lowdown on the Cost Of "Doing Japan"

IN THE EARLY 1960s New Yori's *Village Voice* co-founder and avant-garde columnist John Wilcock showed up in Tokyo with a commission from New York's travel publisher Frommer to do one of its famous $5-a-day books on Japan.

Wilcock did a yoeman's job on the book, and it put Japan on the map as a new destination for the growing horde of backpackers and other budget travelers who had been swarming Europe since the end of World War II, and were beginning to show up in India, Thailand and other Southeast Asian countries.

The good old days when one could actually do Japan on $5 a day have, of course, long since gone (John's book became *Japan on $10 a Day* about a decade later). But, the heart-stopping stories about Tokyo hotels charging $8 for a cup of coffee that began cropping up in the late 1970s, and gave rise to a kind of paranoia about the cost of traveling in Japan, were unfair and have plagued the country's travel industry ever since.

This is not to say that there were no $8 coffees in Japan at that time. There were—and still are! And one could pay as much as $100 for a run-of-the-mill steak dinner—even more for a Buddhist style vegetarian meal in an elite *ryotei* (rio-tay-ee) Japanese style restaurant.

But even in those days, the great majority of Japanese who ate out, as well as the typical traveler, whether Japanese or foreign, did not spend that kind of money for their meals. There were dozens of categories of restaurants, from Chinese, Japanese and Korean to European, where full courses of chicken, fish, meat, vegetables, soup and bread or rice could be had for $6 or $7. There were other restaurants specializing in soba and udon noodles and a variety of rice dishes topped with chicken or beef curry where millions of people ate daily for 75 cents to $1.50.

As for the cost of hotel accommodations, in addition to name brand, luxury class hotels such as the Imperial, the Okura, the New Otani, the Hilton, the Peninsula, the Sheraton, and so on, Japan has long had a much larger number of first-class hotels whose room rates are twenty to forty percent lower than the elites.

And below this selection of first-class hotels, there was, and still is, an even larger number of so-called business-class hotels, which in fact, are often first-class in their facilities and services, that cost from one-third to one-fourth of what brand name hotels charge. Finally, there is a whole national network of strictly budget-class hotels in Japan, with room rates that are lower still.

Then there are Japan's famous *ryokan* (rio-kahn), or inns, of which there are some 70,000 in the country. Many of these inns cater to foreign visitors with packaged rates that make them a viable choice for budget travelers.

Both the image and the reality of Japan being a high-cost travel destination came about because in those days virtually all tourists handled by travel agents were automatically funneled into the most expensive hotels, the most expensive restaurants, and the most expensive modes of travel.

Since the year 2000, hotel room rates have slowly inched up in most of the world's major markets, in some cases far surpassing the rates formerly charged in Japan.

In today's Japan, not only is the cost of hotel accommodations lower than what it was in the 1990s, the number and variety of restaurants is astounding, including virtually every American and European fast food chain you can name, plus dozens of equivalent Japanese chains, and the cost of full Western style meals has plummeted.

Transportation, the third most important cost factor in doing Japan, remains high by American and European standards, but here too, there are options that make it possible to reduce this cost by 30 to 50 percent, by taking advantage of discounted passes available for tourists, by choosing ordinary or express trains rather than super-express trains, by using the marvelous subway system instead of taxis, and for the more adventurous, renting cars.

One can visit and enjoy Japan today without spending a small fortune by the simple process of knowing what accommodations, dining and transportation choices are available, and choosing a level that fits one's budget.

In addition to the cost benefits of eating, traveling, and sleeping like a Japanese citizen, an argument could be made that this would ensure one's experience of "the real Japan" would be far more genuine, enjoyable and satisfying because of more opportunities to interact with the people—who are, after all, one of the country's most important attractions.

Visitors to Japan should make a point of going out of their hotels to eat in "real" Japanese restaurants, particularly those specializing in traditional foods.

-OWARI / END-

Printed in Great Britain
by Amazon.co.uk, Ltd.,
Marston Gate.